STRANDED

STRANDED

Alaska's Worst Maritime Disaster Nearly Happened Twice

AARON SAUNDERS

DUNDURN
TORONTO

Editor: Cheryl Hawley
Design: Courtney Horner
Cover Design: Courtney Horner
Cover image: Aaron Saunders
Back cover image: Library of Congress, Prints and Photographs Division, LC-USZ62-133388
Printer: Webcom

Unless otherwise noted all photos were taken by the author.

Library and Archives Canada Cataloguing in Publication

Saunders, Aaron, 1982-, author
Stranded : Alaska's worst maritime disaster nearly
happened twice / Aaron Saunders.

Includes index.
Issued in print and electronic formats.
ISBN 978-1-4597-3154-7 (paperback).--ISBN 978-1-4597-3155-4 (pdf).--
ISBN 978-1-4597-3156-1 (epub)

1. Princess Sophia (Ship). 2. Star Princess (Ship). 3. Shipwrecks--
Alaska--Pacific Coast. I. Title.

G530.P83S29 2015   909.09164'34   C2015-900899-9
                                                C2015-900900-6

1 2 3 4 5   19 18 17 16 15

We acknowledge the support of the **Canada Council for the Arts** and the **Ontario Arts Council** for our publishing program. We also acknowledge the financial support of the **Government of Canada** through the **Canada Book Fund** and **Livres Canada Books**, and the **Government of Ontario** through the **Ontario Book Publishing Tax Credit** and the **Ontario Media Development Corporation**.

Care has been taken to trace the ownership of copyright material used in this book. The author and the publisher welcome any information enabling them to rectify any references or credits in subsequent editions.
— *J. Kirk Howard, President*

The publisher is not responsible for websites or their content unless they are owned by the publisher.

Printed and bound in Canada.

VISIT US AT
Dundurn.com | @dundurnpress | Facebook.com/dundurnpress |Pinterest.com/dundurnpress

Dundurn
3 Church Street, Suite 500
Toronto, Ontario, Canada
M5E 1M2

To those who love the sea — and those who still make time to read

CONTENTS

INTRODUCTION

O, I have suffered with those that I saw suffer! A brave vessel (Who had no doubt some noble creature in her) Dashed all to pieces! O, the cry did knock against my very heart! Poor souls, they perished!

— William Shakespeare, *The Tempest*

In the course of writing this book, it occurred to me that I can't really remember the first time I learned of the wreck of the *Princess Sophia*. I do, however, remember where I was when I thought it would be a good idea to write a book juxtaposing her accident with the 1995 grounding of the cruise vessel *Star Princess*: in a little pub in Juneau known as the Triangle Club Bar, where I sat, nursing a pint of Alaskan Amber Ale while in port on a cruise through Alaska. I'd come into the bar because I'd heard there was free Wi-Fi internet access with purchase — and there was. But instead of checking emails and filing articles, I found myself staring at a wall covered in photos of famous Alaskan shipwrecks, one of which was the unmistakable silhouette of the *Princess Sophia*, stranded up on Vanderbilt Reef.

The first step in what would become a multi-year journey occurred when I literally walked across the street to Hearthside Books and purchased a copy of Ken Coates and Bill Morrison's masterwork, *The Sinking of the* Princess Sophia. In Alaska, everything you need seems to be close at hand.

I read the book as we made our way up to Skagway, and when I disembarked I stood in the middle of Broadway Street and tried to imagine the scene that would have greeted travellers in October 1918. I found it both easy and difficult; easy because of the cruise ship passengers like myself who swarmed the dock apron and clogged the streets. Difficult because Skagway today is a bit of a parody of itself; there's re-enactments of shootouts and fake brothels designed to entertain families. Have you ever heard a father trying to explain to his son what a brothel is? You will, if you visit Skagway in the summer.

The real tragedy, however, is not that it's difficult to visualize the world of 1918, but that the story of the *Princess Sophia* has been largely forgotten. Even the grounding of the *Star Princess*, which occurred in modern times, wasn't given the media-circus frenzy that has accompanied similar accidents in recent memory. It wasn't until I was one of the hundreds of people queuing up to get back on my massive floating palace in Skagway that it hit me: absolutely no one who comes to Skagway by ship knows the sad, storied events that have played out right in the very waters on which they sail.

Now, you could argue cruise lines don't really want to talk about shipwrecks — it's a bit like showing *Alive* on an airplane. That's fair. But the more I read about both accidents, the more utterly fascinated I became by the parallels between them. The *Princess Sophia* is the *Titanic* of the west coast; yet her journey into obscurity was greatly accelerated by the end of the Great War; the war that, people hoped, would be the War to End All Wars.

Our knowledge of what happened on board during those two grim days *Princess Sophia* spent stranded on Vanderbilt Reef comes from the passengers aboard her, and from those who had the most fleeting encounters with her crew. These included her would-be rescuers who kept their ships nearby in absolutely atrocious weather, sometimes at great risk to their own vessels and personal safety. Passengers wrote letters, some of which were discovered when the ship foundered. Wireless conversations, recorded in Juneau and preserved for all time, also provide brief glimpses into what life was like on board.

Many books about the *Princess Sophia* focus on the trial and the aftermath of the sinking. We don't know every detail of what happened on board, but there's enough witness testimony to put together a substantial part of the puzzle. From there it's possible to fill in the blanks to surmise what exactly happened on board during those two awful days stranded upon Vanderbilt Reef. On the second evening she slipped silently and suddenly into the churning ocean that had been trying to claim her, hidden by a raging snowstorm that only seemed to intensify during her greatest hour of need. She took 343 passengers and crew down with her that night.

At least, we think she did. The official court documents and accident proceedings — which wouldn't be finalized until over a decade after the accident occurred and are contested to this day — continuously pegged the number of souls on board at 343, despite the passenger and crew lists being fraught with errors. Additional crewmembers were brought on board in Skagway to cover for crew who had fallen ill with influenza. They are not recorded on the official list. Many of the Chinese crewmembers who worked aboard the *Princess Sophia* on her final voyage were posthumously (and, today, insensitively) lumped into a single category: "12 Chinamen in steward's department." Either way it's likely there were at least 350 souls on board that final voyage — and that the exact final number will never be known.

If the lists of souls on board could best be described as inaccurate, deciphering a timeline of events in the sinking of the *Princess Sophia* is almost an exercise in pure torture. Alaskan Standard Time is one hour behind Pacific Standard Time that Victoria and Vancouver use. To complicate matters, despite the fact that she spent the majority of her time in Alaskan waters, *Princess Sophia*'s clocks were continually set one hour ahead, on Pacific Standard Time.[1] To help keep things organized, I've standardized all times to Alaskan Standard and not Pacific Standard. In most cases, times given are based on either eyewitness accounts, inquiry testimony, or wireless message records. In a few instances, they're close approximations that I've come to by averaging out the different sources of information. In retelling the events that took place both on board and ashore, I've tried to keep things in chronological order. Establishing this order was, once again, a bit of a jigsaw thanks to differences in time and conflicting witness testimony.

The *Star Princess* proved to be a much easier beast to research — though even then, with a full accident report issued in 1997 by the National Transportation Safety Board, questions still remain, and answers are elusive. Twenty years have passed since that incident occurred, and many of the key players have either retired or passed on during that time.

Besides the books and the accident reports and the hundreds upon hundreds of pages of testimony and legal wrangling that went on in courts on both sides of the border for both incidents, seeing really is believing. I'd taken six separate voyages to Alaska in the past decade, but it was only on my seventh voyage that I managed to finally glimpse Vanderbilt Reef. When the ship I was travelling on passed it in the early hours of the morning the sky was still dark. The reef now has a small tower with a beacon on it. According to the *Juneau Empire*, it's apparently a great place to catch halibut.[2]

In all honesty, I have a hard time picturing the *Princess Sophia* sitting on that impossibly small outcrop of rocks. We sailed straight past it, safely, just like every modern cruise ship that travels between Juneau and Skagway during the busy summer Alaska cruise season. I watched from my balcony on the ship as the reef disappeared from view. It was like seeing a ghost. Somewhere, beneath that murky black sea, her remains still lie.

What isn't difficult to picture is the storm. The weather in Alaska changes in a heartbeat, and the winds that whip down Lynn Canal can be ferocious. I've seen many a cruise passenger lose their hat upon departure from Skagway. Even a sunny July departure can drive people back into the warmth of the ship, where they're sheltered from the howling wind. Just like it did in 1918, strong winds frequently slam into cruise ships departing in the late evening and can roar right down Broadway and up into the White Pass.

The dramatic events that befell *Princess Sophia* in Lynn Canal would culminate in the worst maritime disaster in the history of both Alaska and British Columbia. The tragedy that claimed the lives of every man, woman, and child aboard the *Princess Sophia* would be overshadowed mere weeks later by the end of the First World War, their lives forgotten by the jubilation of a world that was happy to finally be at peace.

Perhaps worst of all, a similar disaster would nearly befall a modern cruise ship traversing the same stretch of Lynn Canal some seventy-six years later. On a routine Alaska cruise in the summer of 1995, on an evening completely dissimilar from the raging snowstorm that in part doomed the *Princess Sophia*, and aided by the latest navigation equipment, Princess Cruises' 810-foot-long *Star Princess* had just completed an operational manoeuvre in the middle of the canal, designed to slow her estimated arrival time in Juneau to keep her on schedule. During this mundane course correction, performed in total darkness with no other vessels in sight, another, equally routine, event occurred: a change of watch between the two Alaska state pilots assigned to *Star Princess* during her time in Alaskan waters.

The events that occurred just after two in the morning on June 24, 1995, would threaten more than just her schedule. It would shake her experienced officers and the state-licenced pilot assigned to guide *Star Princess* safely through Alaskan waters, and thrust both Lynn Canal and the *Princess Sophia* into the spotlight again. Despite the fact that *Star Princess* would be treated to a happy ending, the similarities between the two events are the stuff mystery and fiction writers love: Both vessels departed Skagway on the twenty-third day of the month. Both vessels departed in the evening, from almost the same pier, at nearly the same time. Both were new, state-of-the-art ships, with highly competent crews, heading south through Lynn Canal.

Like many unfortunate events, neither was the result of a single, catastrophic error in judgement. They were caused by an intricate chain of events, coincidences, and mistakes so small and insignificant that neither crew realized they were in any danger until they were well past the point of no return. Both felt they could handle the weather; both felt they knew where they were.

This is the story of two ships, two eras, and the skilled men who seriously misjudged North America's deepest fjord.

Aaron Saunders
Vancouver, British Columbia
March 1, 2015

CHAPTER ONE
THE RUSH TO SKAGWAY

1896-1898
SKAGWAY, ALASKA

The *Princess Sophia* and the *Star Princess* were two very different ships, operating at two very different times. One sank with all hands in what would become the worst maritime disaster in the history of Alaska and British Columbia, while the other was spared that ignominious fate — though just barely. That they both encountered danger in the same stretch of Alaska's 140 kilometre-long Lynn Canal is the bond that unites them.

The view at Lynn Canal seems to offer up the perfect postcard picture of Alaska. Enormous mountain ranges border either side, their snow-capped peaks glistening in the sunlight, dwarfing the glistening white superstructures of the cruise ships that regularly ply these waters during the summer months as their guests head "north, to Alaska."

Few will know that Lynn Canal is actually the deepest fjord in North America, extending 610 metres below its picturesque surface. In fact, most cruise-ship passengers will never see some of its most distinctive — and notorious — features. Vanderbilt Reef, Eldred Rock, and Poundstone Rock are typically passed in the wee hours of the night, as ships make their way to and from the gold rush town of Skagway. Tours up the scenic White Pass & Yukon Route Railroad are popular with the tourists, so cruise ships stay in Skagway as late as nine or even ten p.m., sailing into the darkness that envelops the canal as they begin their return journey south to Juneau.

The winds that blow through Lynn Canal can be fierce, developing out of nowhere and striking with surprising intensity. The surrounding mountains offer little protection from these gusts, which race up the canal and slam into the town of Skagway. On these days, where the wind whips at your face and churns up dust and debris along the waterfront of the town that Jefferson Randolph "Soapy" Smith used to rule in its heyday, the conditions faced by the crews that brought the prospectors, and later tourists, up Lynn Canal can be fully understood.

Skagway Harbor as seen in 1916. The basic layout of the harbour remained largely unchanged from 1898 until the end of the Second World War.

The White Pass & Yukon Route railroad was completed in 1900 and originally ran between Whitehorse and Skagway. Today it makes tourist runs up to Carcross, Yukon Territory, and back — sometimes still using traditional steam power.

Like any disaster, the *Princess Sophia* tragedy has more than one facet. Compounding the remoteness of Skagway and the ever-changing weather conditions in Lynn Canal was how quickly travelling up the canal became a necessity. Few lighthouses were installed until well after 1900, and regulations governing cargo, passengers, and even the vessels themselves couldn't be drawn up as fast as the passenger trade grew.

Today cruise ships plying Alaskan waters are harshly regulated, so much so that John Binkley, the head of the

Alaska Cruise Association, famously quipped in 2008 that pumping the state's own drinking water into the ocean would constitute pollution under the 2006 regulations governing the discharge of grey water and effluent.[1]

At the height of the gold rush, the passenger-ship trade was a completely different story. Regulations were few and far between, and certainly no one on land or at sea was terribly concerned with the consequences of pollution. They were, however, concerned with that other *P* word: *profit.* And in the last dying years of the nineteenth century there was no shortage of profit to be made in Alaska. Many called it "the rush," but the truth of the matter was that a single discovery on a lazy Sunday morning sparked an all-out frenzy that would consume much of the Klondike for decades to come.

On Sunday, August 16, 1896, three prospectors travelling down Rabbit Creek in the Klondike suddenly struck it rich, finding four dollars' worth of gold while engaging in the mundane task of washing their dishes in the stream near their campsite. Knowing an opportunity when they saw it, Skookum Jim, his nephew Charlie Dawson, and brother-in-law George Carmack staked their claims the very next day at the police outpost at Fortymile River. Fuelled by a modest network of explorers and prospectors who were all in the area at the same time, word travelled south with surprising speed. Based on nothing more than word-of-mouth stories passed down from one prospector to another, claims on Rabbit Creek were snatched up by the end of that month. Few who bought in went home disappointed; the pay streak was so rich that the prospectors figured a name change was in order. Almost overnight, Rabbit Creek became Bonanza Creek.

The success prospectors found on Bonanza Creek alone might have been enough to spark a gold rush, but when gold was discovered on nearby Eldorado Creek — and in larger quantities than those present along Bonanza — it created an all-out frenzy across the United States and Canada that spurred people to head north in droves. They were lured to Alaska and the Yukon by visions of untold wealth literally resting on the surface of riverbeds (indeed, some of it was). By the summer of 1897 the Klondike gold rush was in full swing. Demand for travel north was outstripping supply by a long shot, and for most would-be prospectors a single dilemma stood between them and the biggest payday in history: how to get there.

To say that Alaska and the Yukon in the late 1800s were the epitome of the Wild West is an understatement. In order to facilitate the gold rush, entire towns went up overnight. Places like Dawson City, Dyea, and Skagway simply didn't exist before 1897. In 1898 Dawson City had a population of 40,000 inhabitants; the year before just a handful of homesteaders had staked their claims there. Skagway, once a small collection of humble shacks on a beach known as "Mooresville," had nearly 10,000 residents by that summer, along with a main street, hotels, saloons, and the one of the highest concentration of brothels for miles around. Entire towns were being developed faster than law-enforcement officials could keep up with them, leading Samuel Steele of the Royal Canadian Mounted Police to describe Skagway during the height of the gold rush as "little better than a hell on earth."[2] Prospectors coming ashore could expect to be greeted by any number of con men, swindlers, and outright crooks, while those

Skagway in 1897, before the gold rush, bears little resemblance to the town that would pop up literally overnight. At this time it was a small beachhead camp known as Mooresville.

fighting for a space on the returning ships were lucky if they made it on board with their findings intact, having run Skagway's unrelenting gauntlet of brothels, bars, and rigged gambling houses. Gunfights in broad daylight were common, and pistols were practically a prerequisite.

Simply obtaining passage from places like Seattle and Vancouver to the relative lawlessness up north was often as dangerous an experience as the early pioneer towns were themselves. To capitalize on the increasing demand for steamship travel north, anything that could float was pressed into the lucrative passenger trade streaming to and from Alaska, and operators were free to set fares as they saw fit. With little to no regulatory oversight, unscrupulous operators sprang up like the mosquitoes that tormented so many Alaskans, eager to suck them dry at every turn. In 1896 passage on a tramp steamer heading north could cost as much as $40 (roughly $1,100 in modern currency) for a private cabin between Seattle, Juneau, and Dyea, or a bargain $25 if you wanted to travel in a steerage berth. Those fares would nearly triple by the winter of 1897. But all was not lost; for that price you could also bring on 150 pounds of free baggage.[3]

Aboard these semi-derelict ships — many of which had been laid up for years before being pressed into service in 1897 — maximum passenger limits were blatantly disregarded, and vessels were often crewed by a motley assortment of drunks and seamen of dubious distinction in order to get paying customers to the gold as quickly as possible.

The *Clara Nevada* was one such ship. Built in 1871, the 151-foot-long vessel made only one voyage north, in late January 1898. The *Clara Nevada* was well past her prime, having served the United States Coast and Geodetic Survey (USCGS) as the *Hassler* between 1872 and 1897. Her subsequent purchase and refit by the Pacific & Alaska Transportation Company (PATC) had seemingly involved little more than changing the name on her bows and slapping a coat of white paint on her hull. But the Maguire Brothers — the shady duo behind the PATC — were intent on getting her into service as quickly as possible, before the competition found out. Purchasing her for a fraction of her total worth in July 1896, the Maguire Brothers insisted the payment take place via mail so as to avoid any unwanted publicity.[4]

For anyone paying attention, all the warning signs that this was going to be a disastrous maiden voyage were there. Upon backing out of her berth in Seattle on January 26, 1898, she immediately ran full astern into the revenue cutter *Grant*, scraping her hull along the length of the other ship in a shower of sparks and steel screaming in protest before simply continuing on her way into Puget Sound as if nothing had happened. Fights among the crew — most of whom were reportedly drunk on a round-the-clock basis — were commonplace, and passengers found their accommodation to be completely unsuitable. Things had deteriorated so much on board that several passengers had a petition drawn up and ready to be presented by the time the ship reached Port Townsend, Washington, in order to convince customs officials to place them aboard another ship. That probably wasn't a hard sell; witnesses report that the *Clara Nevada* crashed into the pier at Port Townsend as she came alongside.

The ship was in such poor mechanical condition that it took her captain, C.H. Lewis — a man who, months before, had made a dubious name for himself by trying unsuccessfully to sail a wooden paddle steamer out into the open Pacific in pursuit of gold — nearly two hours to successfully berth his ship once she had arrived in Skagway. Owing to the fact that the ship's bridge-to-engine-room telegraphs were no longer operational, Lewis had to bark orders across the deck to another officer, who in turn yelled at the chief engineer, who then shouted commands down to the second engineer who mechanically controlled the ship from the engine room. If passenger reports that the officers and engineers were continually drunk throughout the voyage north are taken at face value, the situation on deck likely bordered on the absurd as the *Clara Nevada* moved repeatedly in and out of port in Skagway, trying unsuccessfully to dock. Once again, docking manoeuvres seemed to be completed only once the ship had physically struck the dock, just as she had back in Port Townsend.

The *Hassler* in one of the only surviving photographs of her short life as *Clara Nevada*. She would go to the bottom of Lynn Canal in February 1898.

These reports are only known due to the few lucky passengers who eventually disembarked in Skagway, blissfully unaware of the dangerous situation they'd just escaped. On the evening of February 5, 1898, as the *Clara Nevada* made her way back down the turbulent waters of Lynn Canal on her first southbound voyage to Seattle, Captain C.H. Lewis sailed her straight into a near-hurricane-force blizzard that raced through the mountain ranges of Lynn Canal and barrelled down on the ship with enormous force. Several witnesses remember seeing her deck lights through the blowing snow as she sailed south down Lynn Canal near Eldred Rock. Without warning, a fireball erupted into the night sky. It tinted the snow and ambient light a ghostly amber colour for miles around. When it had dissipated, the *Clara Nevada* was nowhere to be found.

Speculation still rages to this day as to the exact cause of her sinking. There's substantial evidence to indicate her boilers were in a dangerous state of disrepair and liable to explode at any time. If they did, it might have sparked another, equally devastating, chain of events, since the *Clara Nevada* was rumoured to have also been carrying large quantities of dynamite; a strict "no-no" for vessels in passenger service, even in the lax regulations of 1898. Maintenance was not likely to have been the crew's first priority, and there was the inescapable fact that the *Clara Nevada* had drunkenly bumped and crashed her way north.

More sinister speculation also can't be ignored. *Clara Nevada* was thought to have been carrying as much as $300,000 in gold. Though figures vary wildly, and no one seems to agree on what form it was shipped in, the *Clara Nevada* likely was transporting gold, which was never found despite the wreck lying in relatively shallow waters off Eldred Rock. Accusations that her inexperienced and morally dubious crew had intentionally wrecked the *Clara Nevada* in order to make off with her cargo seem far-fetched, but have persisted for over a century — largely due to the fact that it can't be disproven. Not a single soul who was on board that night is known to have survived.

The tale of the *Clara Nevada*, sadly, is not all that unique — except in that her story is still known to many southeast Alaskans. She was one of many ships to go to the bottom of Lynn Canal during the untamed days of the Klondike gold rush, the vast majority of which have long since vanished into obscurity.

For all those who went to Skagway in search of untold wealth, the vast majority left penniless. J. Bernard Moore, who became one of the first pioneer settlers in Skagway (he initially named the beachhead "Mooresville" after his family name) and who would also be relieved of much of his own fortune later in life, kept a detailed journal of his struggles against the harsh elements in the Klondike. Just weeks before gold was discovered there, on Saturday, July 18, 1896, Moore wrote that his group had been unable to move all day due to unrelenting rain and bitterly cold temperatures.[5] "Still lying here, stormbound," he wrote. "Heavy, cold southerly wind with drizzling rain. I certainly did not expect weather as chilly as this at this season of the year."[6]

The weather — not to mention the mosquitoes — caught many a would-be prospector off guard. The physicality of prospecting also drove others away. Describing his own provisions — which were actually quite sparse for the time — Moore rattles off a laundry list of things that must be carried through the elements: one half-sack of flour, ten pounds of bacon, twenty-five pounds of sugar, fifteen pounds of beans, two small cans of yeast powder, two rolls of butter, two pounds of coffee, five pounds dried mixed fruit, and five pounds of rice.[7]

At the height of the gold rush, between 1897 and 1899, the prices of even the most basic supplies soared. Mediocre horses could fetch as much as $700 — over $20,000 in 2014 currency, and merely getting to the Klondike cost the average person more than a mid-sized car would today.[8] Fewer than four thousand prospectors found gold, and those who did frequently lost their fortunes in subsequent years or spent it all on grandiose (and often bizarre) gestures. Bill Gates — the frontiersman, not the software tycoon of the same name

— earned his place in Dawson City lore when he reportedly presented a local dance hall girl, a nineteen-year-old named Gussie Lamore, with her exact weight in gold.[9] To keep the competition away from his beloved Dawson City, he also famously bought up every available egg in town to ensure that would-be prospectors would lack basic provisions.

The gold rush ended in late 1899. Towns like Skagway and Dawson City gradually became less lawless and started to diversify their economic offerings, while gold was found in other parts of Alaska. The transient prospectors who had come to the Klondike went with it, always in search of an even bigger payday.

By October 1918 the Klondike gold rush had been over for nineteen years. Both Dawson City and Skagway still retained permanent populations, though their numbers were far from those of the boom days of 1898. Dyea had boasted between five and eight thousand inhabitants in 1898, and by 1903 that number had dropped to less than a dozen.[10] In towns like Skagway that had managed to struggle through the post-gold rush hangover, the population was largely seasonal, with only the heartiest "sourdoughs" choosing to stay behind to weather the dark loneliness of the Alaskan winter.

Marine transportation in the autumn of 1918 was scheduled, regulated, and reliable, and provided towns with necessary provisions, freight, and passenger services. Ships would operate from Vancouver and Seattle up to Skagway, where the eighteen-year-old White Pass & Yukon Route Railroad would take passengers safely to Dawson City, bypassing the old Chilkoot Trail that prospectors had to traverse in 1898. No one went to Dyea anymore; the town had been virtually abandoned since 1902, and was a full-fledged ghost town in 1918.

In late October of 1918 one ship quietly pulled into her berth in Skagway, threw out her lines, and tied up. She didn't crash into the dock as *Clara Nevada* had twenty years earlier, and, in fact, her arrival was wholly unremarkable except for the fact that she was running a little behind schedule.

In both design and quality of her crew, the *Princess Sophia* was far different from the derelict craft that was the *Clara Nevada*. One of four nearly identical sister ships in the coastal service fleet of the Canadian Pacific Railway, she was completed in 1912 and operated the Inside Passage route from Vancouver. Her voyages took her up the coast of Alaska, where she would eventually arrive at Skagway before beginning the return journey south. Like her sisters, she was a popular, if simple, ship. On Wednesday, October 23, 1918, she was also fully booked — the perfect escape for those fleeing the north for the winter. It would be her last sailing of the year, and demand for passage south was so strong that additional berths were added to the ship to keep up with demand. Scheduled to leave at 7:00 p.m., *Princess Sophia*'s departure would be delayed until 10:10 that evening to allow for the additional passengers and cargo to be loaded, and to sort out a rather chaotic situation at the docks when stowaways were discovered on board.[11] Those who were fortunate enough to wave to the bystanders on Skagway's docks that night might have thought differently about their luck as *Princess Sophia* made her way south into the darkness of Lynn Canal, chased by fierce winds and a blinding snowstorm that seemed to get worse with each passing hour.

The only similarity *Princess Sophia* bore to the *Clara Nevada* that night was the fact that she, too, was leaving Skagway forever.

CHAPTER TWO
"A SLOW TRIP THROUGH ALASKA"
— PRINCESS SOPHIA

WEDNESDAY, OCTOBER 23, 1918
SKAGWAY, ALASKA

The last embers of the late October sun had just disappeared behind Face Mountain when the 5:30 p.m. train from Whitehorse chugged its way along the centre of Broadway. Like nearly every other person who crowded Skagway's hotels and bars that cold, wet Wednesday evening, the daily "boat train" was packed with passengers bound for the petite little Canadian Pacific steamship known as the *Princess Sophia*.

Fall was the only time of year when Skagway really came alive again, and it was for all the wrong reasons. If the Klondike gold rush twenty years earlier had brought people to Skagway in droves, the winter of 1918 was driving them away. The population in Skagway had had a seasonal quality to it since the gold rush ended in 1899; every year a small yet hearty contingent stayed behind to brave the wind and the cold and the darkness. Not to mention the snow. The deep, thick, never-ending snow that made roads impassable and periodically stopped the trains between Skagway and Carcross, despite the best efforts of the rotary plow that was sometimes buried up to its cab. It's no wonder that those with the means to travel south each year did so, preferring to winter elsewhere and return to Skagway in the spring when temperatures had warmed up. Those who stayed on throughout the dark Alaskan winter remained, ostensibly, out of an undying love for their community; though it's equally likely they could not afford to book passage themselves.

That year, the fall exodus seemed more pronounced. Like a nail in the coffin, the last ship of the season marked the official start of the long winter ahead — and this would be the last time that *Princess Sophia* would grace Skagway with her presence. More than usual, people in Skagway seemed to not only notice, but understand this. Hotels were packed, and cargo — which would eventually total 266 pieces ranging from horses to Christmas presents to war supplies — was already clogging the pierside sheds, with dock workers trying desperately to keep up with the continuous stream of supplies.

Pre-departure festivities held in Skagway went on unabated for nearly a full week. The evening of Saturday, October 19 was noticeably more festive than in years past, with *The Daily Alaskan* proclaiming the annual Sourdough Dance held that night, "one of the most enjoyable affairs ever held in Skagway."[1] The paper, run by L.S. Keller, was the only source of news in Skagway following the shutdown of the *Skaguay News* in 1904. Additional parties continued throughout the week: on Monday evening the White Pass Athletic Club threw a dance in honour of those heading south, and Tuesday evening brought with it a large fund-raiser put on by the Skagway Popular Picture Palace to refurbish St. Mark's Church. Once again, Keller's paper waxed nostalgic about the event, which featured the "rich baritone voice" of a Mr. William O'Brien of Dawson City. O'Brien was no stranger to Skagway — indeed, *The Daily Alaskan* billed him as the man who "hardly needs an intro-duction." This time, though, he was in town for a limited engagement: along with his wife and five children, William O'Brien was due to set sail on *Princess Sophia* the following evening, like so many others in town that night. By the time *The Daily Alaskan* came off the press Wednesday morning, the jubilation of the night before had already evaporated, replaced with a town filled with travellers anxious to board the *Princess Sophia* and finally get underway.

One such person was twenty-five-year-old Walter Harper, who was travelling with his wife, Frances, on a one-way trip to Philadelphia. Harper had gained notori-ety, at the young age of twenty-one, after becoming the first person to successfully ascend Mount McKinley on June 7, 1913, along with fellow climbers Harry Karstens,

Hudson Stuck, and Robert Tatum. Even after achieving such a monumental feat, things were still looking up for the young mountaineer. He'd survived a frightening bout with typhoid fever in 1916 and just a few weeks before sailing, on September 1, 1918, he'd married Frances Wells — the nurse who had treated him at Fort Yukon's Mission Hospital. Now, Harper and his new wife were bound for the east coast, where he had been accepted into medical school in Philadelphia. The arduous but enjoyable journey ahead would serve as their honeymoon.

Others gathered on the docks in Skagway for far less glamorous reasons. A total of eighty-seven passengers — all employees of the White Pass & Yukon Route Railroad and the American Yukon Navigation Company — were making the journey south. They were steamboat men, having just finished their contracts on board the steamers that ran seasonally along the Yukon River from Whitehorse to St. Michael and back. Four of the men were certified master mariners, while the others ranged from deckhands to cabin stewards. With their work done and their ships tied up for the season, they too were headed south to escape the winter freeze-up.

Booking passage south in 1918 was far from being an exact science. For those employed on a seasonal basis — as nearly everyone was — changing schedules had a way of creating absolute chaos with passenger lists. Ships that were booked full one day suddenly had available berths the next day, and vice-versa. The *Princess Sophia* was a well-liked vessel among northerners, and many passengers went out of their way to book their tickets aboard her in advance. Even in the days leading up to her departure, it was unclear exactly how many people would be travelling aboard the *Princess Sophia*.

Confusion wasn't merely limited to a few latecomers whose plans had changed. In fact, so many last-minute travellers had turned up in Skagway looking for passage south that those who lacked tickets (and nearly everyone did) suddenly became priority number one for the shipping lines. As early as October 17, while *Princess Sophia* was still in tied up in Vancouver, Canadian Pacific's Skagway agent, Lewis H. Johnston, telegraphed word that between six and seven hundred ticketless passengers had already arrived in town, and were all eager to get out of Skagway before the winter freeze-up. The fall exodus was among the most lucrative for Canadian Pacific, and Johnston advised that if Canadian Pacific could squeeze more berths onto *Princess Sophia* for her last run south, he would have no issues selling them immediately — presumably at a premium.

Four years earlier, adding additional berths would have been a walk in the park. But in the early morning hours of Monday, April 15, 1912, the largest ship in the world — White Star Line's RMS *Titanic* — had foundered in the North Atlantic after striking an iceberg, taking more than 1,500 souls down with her. Her loss had changed the way maritime authorities regulated lifesaving equipment on board, which would no longer be measured by tonnage but instead by the maximum number of passengers on board.

Based on Johnston's wire to the company, Canadian Pacific determined they could add an additional fifty berths to the *Princess Sophia* before she set out on her last northbound trip to Skagway. To account for the increase in overall passenger capacity, extra life rafts were quickly installed at the same time. They were stacked, one atop the other, on the roof of her smoking room, next to the lifeboats mounted in davits. The new rescue craft were made of wood and not steel like *Princess Sophia*'s existing boats. They were, for all intents and purposes, merely window dressing; reassurances that, if an emergency were to occur, all passengers and crew on board would be able to safely abandon ship. As they were hoisted aboard the *Princess Sophia* pierside in Vancouver, few if any of the workers or crew supervising the installation of these new craft ever seriously thought they would be needed.

Even with the additional berths installed before the last voyage north, numerous people were still turned away on sailing day in Skagway. Edward Bemis, a purser who served aboard the riverboat *Tanana*, was one of them. He had wired ahead in advance to Skagway to secure his passage south aboard the *Princess Sophia*, but discovered upon arrival that Canadian Pacific simply didn't have enough space aboard her. Placed on the *Prince Rupert*, he and his fellow travellers tried to goad several confirmed *Princess Sophia* passengers into transferring their tickets to them, without success. Resigned to the fact they would be heading out aboard the *Prince Rupert*, Bemis wished his friends on the *Princess Sophia* farewell. "'We'll see you in Seattle' was the general remark as we left," he would later say. "It never occurred to any of us that we were saying goodbye for the last time."[2]

Those who did manage to secure passage aboard the *Princess Sophia* were as diverse as the north itself — and not all who came were excited about the journey south. Travelling from Dawson City, Murray and Lulu Mae Eads

Skagway, 2014. Except for the modern cruise ships in the foreground and the new pier structure, little has changed. Departure from Skagway today looks nearly as it would have in 1918.

were booked on the *Princess Sophia*, destined for Seattle. They had each paid $37.50 for their first-class passage, and were travelling south after selling their business interests in Dawson City. Lulu Mae was a dance-hall singer who, despite having been charged with "allowing women of loose, idle or suspicious character on the premises for the purpose of drinking and keeping company with men,"[3] was well liked in Dawson City.

She was also deathly afraid of the voyage south. Since coming to Alaska from Alabama in the early 1900s, she'd never once sailed south for the winter; a highly uncommon situation for northerners with as much money on hand as

Lulu Mae. Now, with a journey that would take them by sea to Seattle then along the Pacific Coast and through the Panama Canal by ship, the Eads had a Dawson City lawyer modify their wills: if both of them should die together, their estate was to be split equally amongst Lulu Mae's two sisters.

As Murray and Lulu Mae Eads stared out the window of their train coach, darkened trees giving way to houses and buildings on the approach to Skagway, there was likely no shortage of anxiety between the couple. The long journey from Dawson must have been nearly intolerable; the safety and security they had known in the north for nearly two decades was evaporating with each passing mile.

Even the train that brought them to Skagway along the famed White Pass & Yukon Route wasn't exactly inspiring confidence in the worried travellers. The twenty-eight-year-old railway hadn't purchased a single new piece of equipment since 1908, and the existing passenger cars were becoming worn from overuse and caked with the fine, granulated black soot that belched from the locomotive as it slowed to a crawl in the cold night rain.

Like ants swarming out of a hill, passengers rushed off the Pullman cars across the pier, to the relative warmth and splendour of the *Princess Sophia*. She was never Canadian Pacific's most glamorous ship — that award went to the sleek, white-hulled *Empress* fleet that plied the Pacific Ocean. But with her deck lights glowing in the ever-increasing darkness, she shone across the docks like a beacon of hope.

Built in Paisley, Scotland, at the Bow, McLaughlan and Company shipyard, *Princess Sophia* was on the verge of celebrating her seventh birthday. She had been officially launched on November 8, 1911, when her hull met the waters of Scotland's famous Clyde River for the first time. At a contract price of £51 million she was the second ship to have been built by Bow and McLaughlan for Canadian Pacific. Stout and sturdy, she was designed exclusively for Canadian Pacific's Alaskan runs between Vancouver and Skagway, but could be deployed elsewhere if need be. Indeed, capacity needs sometimes found her doing short overnight jaunts between Vancouver and Victoria. With four passenger decks and a single tall, buff-and-black funnel centred nearly amidships, her two-hundred-forty-five-foot length and forty-four-foot beam gave her a decidedly unique exterior profile.

Designed specifically to handle the unpredictable winter weather of the west coast, *Princess Sophia* proved her seaworthiness on her delivery run. She set sail from Greenock, Scotland on February 12, 1912, and arrived in Victoria, British Columbia, over three months later, on May 20. Her journey had taken her across the Atlantic Ocean, around Cape Horn and the dreaded Drake Passage, and up the western coasts of South and North America.

On that cold October evening in Skagway, *Princess Sophia* arrived like a well-known old friend. Embarking passengers battling for a spot on the gangway were no doubt looking forward to settling in to their staterooms for the voyage south. Thirty-one-year-old Ilene Winchell boarded the *Princess Sophia* to discover that she was already on the deck where her stateroom was located. She occupied Stateroom 35 on the aft port side of awning deck. It was one of the better accommodations on board, as it had a porthole window that could be opened to let the fresh air in.

Her neighbour wouldn't be so fortunate; immediately adjacent to Ilene's room was Stateroom 33 — a small interior room with no natural daylight. To make her journey more comfortable, Winchell had booked a room with a view. Her room was also conveniently located: the shared water closet that held toilet and showering facilities was located in the small alcove that housed her stateroom, along with Staterooms 33 and 37. But although there were two berths in her cozy Stateroom 35, she would need only one.

Winchell had left her husband, Al, behind in Iditarod, Alaska — a small town of barely fifty inhabitants situated along the Iditarod River to the northwest of Anchorage. Gold had been discovered in nearby Flat, Alaska, in 1910, and Al Winchell was employed — suitably — by the Yukon Gold Company. But his wife's journey south wasn't because their marriage was crumbling; it was due to Ilene's prolonged ill health that would surely be exacerbated by the coming winter. Rather than suffer through another brutal Alaskan winter that could only leave her in an increasingly weakened state, Al had suggested that Ilene travel south to recuperate in the warmer California climate. Paying $37.50 for her ticket, she had booked passage to Seattle aboard *Princess Sophia*. From there she would transfer to her connections to California. In the spring, when temperatures had improved, she would return north to Iditarod and her husband.

Parting for an entire season would have been difficult in normal circumstances, but Ilene Winchell's personal circumstances were anything but ordinary. In addition to her illness, which sapped her energy and left her weak, she had spent the better part of the days and weeks leading up to her journey to Skagway obsessing over premonitions of her impending death. She was so convinced she would die that she even told her husband, "I can't tell you how I know it, but you will outlive me." Hoping to reassure his wife, Al Winchell reminded her that she was travelling on one of the newest Canadian Pacific steamships, and that her entire journey from Iditarod to California would be a perfectly safe one. Unsatisfied, Ilene Winchell made her husband promise that if the worst should happen he would find and bury her remains next to her mother. Hoping to calm his wife's irrational fears, Al Winchell agreed.

By the time she had reached Skagway, Ilene Winchell was so weak from the journey that she was personally escorted to Stateroom 35 by a member of the ship's crew. It had a white slatted door with a small brass number plate with her stateroom number pressed into it above the door. Opening the door, Winchell found the electric lights burning brightly, glinting off the highly polished woodwork on the two berths and illuminating the smart-looking white walls. Exhausted after the long journey to Skagway, Winchell likely settled into an uneasy sleep; one punctuated by the sounds of footsteps in the corridor as the rest of *Princess Sophia*'s passengers embarked for the voyage south.

By and large, *Princess Sophia* was a very comfortable ship; a sort of transatlantic ocean liner in miniature. Although her public rooms lacked the grandeur of Canadian Pacific's much larger steamers, they were akin to staying in a fine, boutique hotel. When she was launched in 1912, the *Paisley Gazette* of Paisley, Scotland, raved about the new ship their town had produced:

Last Saturday, the new steamer "Princess Sophia" left the Clyde on her voyage across the Atlantic to take up her place in the Canadian Pacific Railway company's fleet. Reference was made in the "Town Talk" column last week to the majestic appearance of the vessel as she left the Cart to engage in her trials, and a correspondent's regret that a photograph of her was not published in the "Gazette" has resulted in several snap-shots coming to hand this week. A full account of the launching ceremony and speeches, with photographs, was published here at the time the vessel took to the water in the month of November. The Princess Sophia is the largest-engined vessel that ever was built on the Cart. She is 245 feet long and has cost between £50,000 and £60,000, of which some £40,000 went in wages in Paisley. She is specifically designed for passenger service on the Pacific coast.[4]

Although designed for the less-glamorous runs of the Pacific, *Princess Sophia*'s interior spaces were noteworthy for their connection to the sea: nearly all featured windows that looked out onto the vessel's promenade decks or out onto the landscape of the ocean beyond the hull. Even the ship's main staircase featured an attractive skylight designed to filter natural light down into the deeper recesses of the hull.

The social hub of life on board the *Princess Sophia* was the aptly named social hall on awning deck. Located at the forward end of the ship, adjacent to many of her passenger accommodations, the social hall was attractively panelled in white with dark wooden accents. At its after end the social hall was bookended by the ship's main staircase, or what would be called the grand staircase on a much larger ocean liner. An attractive wooden staircase lined with ornately carved railings, it led up to the ship's promenade deck, which featured additional passenger accommodations, outdoor deck space, and an attractive observation room, finished in maple, located all the way forward. From the lounge, passengers aboard the *Princess Sophia* could admire the view over her bow; one that was not all that dissimilar from what her officers would see one deck above in the ship's bridge.

Meals aboard the *Princess Sophia* were taken in several sittings in the ship's dining room, which was lined with oversized windows and decorated with the finest mahogany and maple. Up to one hundred guests could be seated here at a single time, at long tables featuring wooden chairs with leather backings. Unlike some of the newer ocean liners, these chairs were of the "old-school" variety: they were still bolted to the floor to keep them from sliding around in inclement weather, and swivelled atop a brass pedestal.

All the way at the stern on promenade deck was the ship's clubby smoking room. Situated in a deck house separated from the main structure of the ship, the smoking room was the domain of the first-class gentlemen on board the *Princess Sophia*, and her interiors reflected that masculine ideal. Like the dining room, the smoking room was finished with mahogany and maple accent panels, and adorned with a variety of leather-backed chairs and couches. It oozed the smell of leather, scotch, and tobacco.

Passengers typically stayed in one of a handful of accommodation types. First-class passengers were all accommodated in cabins situated on promenade deck and awning deck, with additional cabins situated high up on the boat deck, just aft of the ship's wheelhouse. Unlike their counterparts on promenade and awning decks, these boat deck staterooms had no interior corridor access; passengers had to walk outside onto the open deck, cross down to promenade deck, and re-enter the ship there.

Even these guests still did better than *Princess Sophia*'s second-class passengers, twenty-seven of whom were relegated to a common accommodations area on main deck, the lowest passenger-accessible deck on the ship.

Fares for the passage south were far more uniform, with first-class guests paying $37.50 per person for passage to Vancouver, Victoria, or Seattle; and $20.00 to travel as far as Prince Rupert, British Columbia. Employees of the White Pass & Yukon Route were given a sizeable discount of $12.50 per person, which brought individual fares down to an even $25.00. In modern currency, $37.50 is approximately $595.38 — the cost of a domestic transcontinental flight.

Second-class passengers paid far less. With all but four guests continuing on to Seattle, most passengers paid $22.00 per person, while the three individuals who were only travelling as far as Prince Rupert paid just $11.00 a head. With first class full up, it's likely that some of those booked in second class might have travelled first class under normal circumstances. With berthing spaces so scarce, and winter closing in, few would-be travellers had the luxury of being particular.

In command of *Princess Sophia* on her last southbound voyage from Skagway was Captain Leonard Pye Locke. A capable and competent mariner, the sixty-six-year-old

Locke joined the Canadian Pacific Steamship Company in 1901, after what could best be termed a lifetime at sea. Born in 1852 in Halifax, Nova Scotia, Locke had joined his father — also a mariner — at sea in 1868, when he was just sixteen years old.

His early days with Canadian Pacific seem to have been successful, at least financially. In 1906 Locke and his wife, Emily, had a new house constructed for them in Victoria, at 1005 Cook Street. [5] The one-and-a-half-storey Edwardian front-gabled house was typical of the style at the time, with large bay windows on the main level that looked out onto a wraparound porch. With a red-brick chimney slowly dispersing smoke into the air from the household fireplace, the home was warm, cozy, and inviting for Emily and her five children. Locke, however, was seldom there to enjoy it.

Stout in appearance, Leonard Locke was a man of average height, with a prominent face sporting a large, bushy moustache beginning to show the first signs of grey. That he wore a toupée is the most colourful piece of information that survives about him. Like most competent mariners who successfully sail their vessels from one port to another, Locke's career up until October 1918 had been largely unremarkable. Pressed later, crew members who had served under him could only come up with the most basic of statements to describe his personality. Some said he was strict — perhaps unsurprising for an early twentieth-century sea captain. Others simply remembered him as being fastidious. A few close friends remarked that the captain bore a great fondness for the poetry of Robert Service.

Despite having served nearly eighteen years with the company, there is only one anecdote that offers the most fleeting glimpse of Leonard Locke, the man. J.L McPherson of the Seattle Chamber of Commerce sailed aboard one of *Princess Sophia*'s northbound voyages in 1917, and he kept as a memento a copy of a poem that Locke had written for a young girl who was on board. The girl had been upset that no one had come to see her off when the ship sailed from Vancouver, and that she had no friends on board. Locke wrote the poem specifically for her, and ensured it was placed next to her dinner plate that evening.

Little moments like that, however, were far from Locke's mind as *Princess Sophia* finally came alongside in Skagway. The aging sea captain was acutely aware that the ship's scheduled departure time of 7:00 p.m. was looking increasingly unlikely. The voyage north had presented Locke with several pressing concerns, and he set his mind on solving them.

After arriving in Skagway at 1:00 p.m., the crew hurried about the business of turning the ship around for her voyage south to Vancouver. During this time Captain Locke, clad in his uniform, personally trudged through the rain to the offices of Lewis Johnston, Canadian Pacific's agent in Skagway. Located on Broadway, adjacent to the bizarre driftwood-clad building that housed the Fraternal Order of the Arctic Brotherhood, Locke's visit was for an unusual reason: four of *Princess Sophia*'s deckhands and two stewards had come down with influenza, an epidemic of which was sweeping through North America in 1918. This was, Locke hoped, the last in a long line of problems, delays, and minor annoyances that had beset the ship since she sailed from Vancouver on October 17.

When *Princess Sophia* arrived at Alert Bay, her first port of call on the voyage north, Captain Locke received an SOS from the Alaskan Steamship Company vessel *Alaska*. As she made her way south, the *Alaska* had run aground near Swanson Bay, stranding her complement of three hundred passengers on board. Since Swanson Bay was en route to *Princess Sophia*'s next port of call in Prince Rupert, Locke left Alert Bay early and steamed rapidly toward the scene. As if to demonstrate just how changeable the tides and weather conditions were in the area at the time, when *Princess Sophia* arrived on the scene the *Alaska* had already managed to free herself. Indeed, upon their arrival in Prince Rupert, the *Alaska* could be seen at dock, smoke drifting lazily from her single funnel while throngs of passengers disembarked like ants running through a maze.

Time lost to this diversion was made up on the way to Juneau, where *Princess Sophia* arrived on the evening of Tuesday, October 22, 1918. Thick clouds obliterated the treeline of Mount Roberts, which was situated near the docks. A steady rain fell, and the *Princess Sophia*, her lights aglow, came alongside a sleepy town tucked in for the evening. Up until then the ship had been almost entirely empty for the voyage north. With winter approaching, only the heartiest — or craziest, depending on who you talked to — folks were actually heading up north.

One man, however, did come in out of the rain and step onto the brightly lit decks of the *Princess Sophia* while she was docked in Juneau. Customs Collector John Pugh was travelling as a non-revenue passenger up to Skagway, where he planned to assist with the crushing mob of people looking for passage south. As bad as it was, the issue of

The Arctic Brotherhood Hall. Built in 1899, it now houses the Skagway visitor's centre. The Canadian Pacific Steamship Company offices were located just next door in 1918, in the blue-and-white building that now houses one of Skagway's many jewellery stores.

the passengers was almost secondary to the issue of cargo; with Christmas just around the corner, Pugh knew the task ahead would be gargantuan on both fronts. He was scheduled to sail with the *Princess Sophia* back to Juneau, where he would disembark on Thursday.

Then there was the issue of the flu outbreak on board. But Locke needn't have worried about finding suitable applicants willing to leave Skagway on a moment's notice at this time of year. As quickly as he had arrived at the Canadian Pacific office in Skagway, the portly sea captain

Juneau, Alaska, in the early 1900s. This is where Customs Collector John Pugh embarked *Princess Sophia* on the evening of Tuesday, October 22, 1918, and where she was destined to arrive on the morning of Thursday, October 24, 1918.

Library of Congress, Prints & Photographs Division, LC-DIG-ppmsc-02102.

found himself walking briskly back up Broadway toward his ship with ten new men in tow. For the new hires, it's highly probable that this was a spirited walk filled with hollers and calls out to friends; six of Locke's newest recruits had been poached right from the White Pass & Yukon Route Railroad's complement of waiters, and the small group would have had to walk across the tracks laid down the centre of Broadway and straight past the WP&YR's offices to get to the piers and their new home on board *Princess Sophia*. They weren't merely leaving Skagway for good: they were moving up to bigger and better things, and likely weren't shy about letting the townspeople know.

Now fully crewed, Captain Locke also took the time to visit Dr. William Gardner Gabie at his office in the White Pass

Broadway Street in Skagway, facing the cruise ship docks. In 1918 the WP&YR tracks would have run clean down the centre of the street, but many of the buildings remain largely unchanged.

Hospital on Broadway and 11th, at around 4:00 p.m. that afternoon.[6] Dr. Gabie's official title was city health officer, which is the polite way of saying he was the only man in town to consult on medical issues.[7] Dr. Gabie had been summoned to the *Princess Sophia* when she had arrived in Skagway to determine the extent of the possible influenza outbreak on board, but was stopped at the top of the gangway by Second Officer Frank Gosse, who refused to let Dr. Gabie embark. Not wishing to risk potentially spreading the disease to the residents of Skagway with winter closing in, Second Officer Gosse offered to orally describe the symptoms of the six ill crewmembers, who were mostly stewards, to Dr. Gabie. "They all took sick about the same time," Gabie would later recall. "They had all taken down with chills and fever and prostration."[8]

Dr. Gabie "gave the officers instructions on how to take care of those patients." Before going back uptown to have influenza treatments prepared by the town druggist and left at the Canadian Pacific offices on Broadway for pickup, he requested Second Officer Gosse "see the Captain," and asked that he be sent up to Gabie's office to discuss the situation on board the *Princess Sophia*.

Gabie had known Captain Locke for many years, and the doctor now welcomed Locke into his office warmly. Their half-hour conversation, however, revolved mainly around the crewmembers who had fallen ill. Locke wasn't particularly frightened of the prospect of an influenza outbreak on board his ship, and Dr. Gabie would later testify that he seemed "just as he always was"[9] during their brief visit. Satisfied that Captain Locke had the situation under control (and reassured that he kept a small provision of "medicinal" rum on board at all times, tucked away under lock and key), Dr. Gabie said goodbye to Captain Locke, who returned to his waiting ship.

Locke himself wasn't immune to health issues. During the winter of 1917 Canadian Pacific Captain Arthur Slater was unexpectedly called in to relieve Captain Locke of his command on board the *Princess Sophia*. Locke had been complaining of ill-health, and head waiter Wolfe Templeman had overheard the captain mention his general discomfort while dining with several passengers at his usual table. Templeman waited on Captain Locke's table from June 30, 1917, until he signed off in April of 1918. He would have the good fortune to not be present on board during *Princess Sophia*'s last trip.

What was causing Locke such difficulty during the winter of 1917 is not known, but it seems to have been temporary. Templeman records that Captain Locke resumed command of *Princess Sophia* from Captain Slater on the following voyage. If his illness the previous winter troubled him at all now, Captain Locke never let on.

When Locke arrived back at his ship, Second Officer Frank Gosse and Third Officer Arthur Murphy seemed to have a handle on the cargo situation. The two men had been working diligently ever since *Princess Sophia* had arrived in Skagway to supervise the offloading of her cargo that was to remain in the north. Now they were in the midst of trying to manoeuvre thirteen horses belonging to Herb McDonald across the dock apron and onto the ship via her exterior shell doors. McDonald had been a fixture in Dawson City for as long as most folks could remember, but he too was heading south for the last time, intending to transport his horses and burgeoning freight business to Vancouver. He looked on with his wife, Emma, as his strong equines were loaded onto the ship under the direction of James Kirk. A pioneer of the 1898 gold rush, Kirk had been hired by McDonald to oversee the transportation of his horses south. Unlike McDonald, however, Kirk fully intended to return to Dawson City at the next available opportunity in order to be with his wife. Even at fifty years of age, Kirk still wasn't finished with the Klondike, and no doubt saw McDonald's offer as a good chance to make some additional money before the lean winter months hit.

McDonald's thirteen made up the majority of the twenty-four horses that would be loaded onto the *Princess Sophia*, but there was one horse that had already attained

Cargo is loaded onto a ship in Cordova, Alaska, in the early 1900s. The scene on the Skagway docks would have been much the same, with cargo and passengers coming and going.

almost mythical status by that night. Walter Barnes, a Dawson-area miner for nearly two decades, was making the trip south solely to accompany his loyal horse, Billy, to a farm in southern British Columbia where he would live out his last days. For eighteen years, the pure-white horse known fondly as "Old Billy" had served Barnes well, pulling carts loaded with gravel and gold through a 1,700-foot-long tunnel day in and day out. The resulting haul of gold had made Barnes a wealthy man, but Billy was now too old to work. Rather than have him sent to the slaughterhouse — or simply left to die on his own, which was not at all uncommon when animals had outlived their usefulness in the north — Barnes arranged to have Old Billy put aboard the *Princess Sophia*. He would make the journey south with his beloved companion and winter at his home in Vancouver before returning to Dawson City the following spring.

Canadian Pacific's Skagway agent, Lewis Hellett Johnston, had also placed five dogs on the cargo manifest. Along with the twenty-four horses they were the only living cargo placed aboard *Princess Sophia* that evening. The animals would turn out to be far less problematic than the other pieces of cargo waiting in the brightly lit sheds. With so many passengers looking upon this voyage not as a journey south but as an *exodus*, the cargo manifest was more varied than usual. Passengers were literally bringing their whole lives with them, regardless of what that entailed. Those who were staying behind to brave the winter in the north were also using *Princess Sophia* as a mail system; she carried with her several tons of Christmas presents destined for friends and relatives down south.

In all, five tons of cargo of varying shapes and sizes would be loaded on board *Princess Sophia* for her southbound voyage, along with passenger baggage marked "Not Wanted On The Voyage" that would be stowed below until arrival in their port of disembarkation. With the late arrival of the White Pass & Yukon Route "boat train" from Whitehorse at 5:30 p.m., the simple act of loading all the baggage the passengers streaming off the train had brought with them and processing it for sailing would take a full hour and a half. Double-checking everything on the manifest was left up to twenty-year-old David Robinson, *Princess Sophia*'s young wireless officer. With little for him to do while his ship was moored, Robinson moonlighted as the ship's freight clerk when she was not at sea.

By 7:00 p.m. most passengers were cleared to begin embarking the *Princess Sophia*. This was where Juneau Customs Collector John Pugh came in. He almost always went by Jack, and was both well-known and well-liked in Juneau, Skagway, and beyond. Enormously popular, he likely knew many of those embarking on *Princess Sophia*. With daylight now gone and the temperature dropping, the coolness of the October air nipped at Pugh as he went about his business, checking papers, and greeting old friends.

Before the ship could sail, one final very important piece of cargo had to be loaded. It was left until nearly the last moment, when the docks had been cleared and most of the guests had embarked. Few had seen it arrive; fewer still even knew of its presence on board the *Princess Sophia*.

The Wells Fargo Banking Company had been serving Alaskan communities since 1883, but in 1918 the United States government had taken control of the company's express service as a wartime measure. Wells Fargo, meanwhile, was in the midst of withdrawing their operations in Alaska to focus on their business farther south.[10, 11] This could partly explain the presence on board *Princess Sophia* of a Wells Fargo safe containing $62,000 in gold bars[12] — roughly $960,000 in modern currency.[13] Because of its highly sensitive nature, it's likely that the safe was personally signed for by Purser Charles Beadle. Since the *Princess Sophia* lacked a dedicated specie room for valuable cargo, Beadle directed the safe to be placed in the ship's chart room, where gold had been stored on past voyages. Along with the safe, four additional bags of mail were also loaded

The scene that would have greeted those making their way to Skagway from the north aboard the WP&YR "boat train" was a bleak one. Outside of small towns like Carcross, civilization wouldn't be seen until they pulled into town.

on board the *Princess Sophia*. But these weren't filled with letters and Christmas toys for the kiddies; instead, they contained another $70,000 in gold. They were placed alongside the safe in the chart room, where the ship's officers could keep personal watch over such valuables.

With all the necessary cargo and provisions on board and the passengers gradually settling into their staterooms, things on board *Princess Sophia* were drawing to their inevitable conclusion as paperwork was wrapped up and well-wishes given. To prepare for departure from Skagway,

Looking north down Broadway Street in Skagway, around 1900. Note the rails running down the centre of Broadway for the White Pass & Yukon Route trains.

805
BROADWAY LOOKING NORTH
SKAGWAY, ALASKA

CALLARMAN

Captain Locke had Chief Engineer Charles H. Walker bring up the steam in the ship's boilers. Walker was filling in for *Princess Sophia's* first engineer, Archibald Alexander, who was granted permission at the last minute to miss the roundtrip sailing from Vancouver when his wife telephoned from Victoria to say that both of Alexander's young children had come down with influenza, and his daughter was not expected to live. Walker, along with two other engineers, would cover Alexander's watch rotations.

Now Walker was doing just that. With a thin jet of black smoke beginning to pour from her funnel, Princess *Sophia* was finally ready to set sail at 10:00 p.m. — three hours behind her scheduled departure time of 7:00 p.m.

Before she departed, Lewis Johnston, Canadian Pacific's man in Skagway, briefly stepped on board *Princess Sophia's* warmly lit deck to confer with Purser Charles Beadle. Both men agreed the process had gone as smoothly as could be reasonably expected, and Johnston wished him a pleasant trip south before ascending one deck to the navigation bridge. There he found Captain Locke readying *Princess Sophia* for departure. Johnston had known Locke for over a decade, and the two men took the chance to catch up, however briefly, and discuss the voyage ahead. Locke was satisfied with how things had gone, both in terms of the newly replaced crewmembers and the loading and offloading of passengers and cargo. At five minutes past ten, Lewis Johnston shook Captain Locke's hand and left the navigation bridge.

Clearly Locke had no issues with the evening's embarkation or the voyage ahead. Lewis Johnston was the last man down the gangway that night. Stepping out into the cold, Johnston hiked up the collar of his greatcoat and exchanged waves with the crew as the gangway was removed from the *Princess Sophia*. He wished them a pleasant season and a safe journey south before he turned his back to the ship and slowly, quietly made his way back up the dimly lit expanse of Broadway Street. The night air chilled him, and he felt exhausted after a long day of work. He returned to his offices on Broadway just long enough to send a message to Captain James Troup, Canadian Pacific's superintendent for the British Columbia coast, stating that *Princess Sophia* had departed shortly after 10:00 p.m. local time with two hundred seventy-eight passengers, twenty-four horses, and five tons of freight on board.

At ten minutes past ten *Princess Sophia* slipped away from the pier on her last voyage south. Her itinerary was an active one. The next day she would call on both Juneau and Wrangell before setting sail for Ketchikan and Prince Rupert, where she would arrive on Friday, October 25. On Saturday the 26th she would come alongside in Alert Bay, and finally, on Sunday, October 26, 1918, she would dock at Canadian Pacific's Pier D at the foot of Granville Street in Vancouver. From there connecting passengers could transfer to the inter-coastal steamers bound for Victoria and Seattle.

For the passengers who were hearty enough to line her rails that night, few tears would be shed as Skagway slowly disappeared off the stern of the *Princess Sophia*. With so many passengers travelling on one-way tickets, they were looking forward to the journey ahead and delighting in the relative novelty of spending their first night on board a ship. By the time she had made her first turn to port and entered into the Taiya Inlet proper, most of *Princess Sophia's* passengers had retreated indoors, lured by the glowing lights of the ship's public rooms and the warmth of their own staterooms. Those

The *Princess Sophia* pulls away from Pier D in Vancouver, bound for Alaska.

who remained on deck would have experienced a sudden blast of cold wind that slammed into her superstructure as she made the turn; a moment all too common for ships sailing south toward the vast expanse of Lynn Canal. Gradually, these few hearty stragglers also retreated back inside.

The cold wind from the north roared into Skagway too, driving onlookers away from Pier D and back to their houses. A few hearty souls wandered aimlessly back to the bars that had been the source of so much life during the gold rush, lamenting the fact that they could no longer treat

Sailing Lynn Canal from Skagway, bound for Juneau. In 1918 the driving snow and fierce winds likely kept most passengers off *Princess Sophia*'s open decks and hid the mountain ranges from view, but those departing aboard *Star Princess* in 1995 would have enjoyed a similar view and weather conditions before retiring for the night.

themselves to the warmth of a liquid sort as they talked about days gone by. Alaska's own prohibition law, dubbed the "Bone Dry" law, had begun at the start of 1918.

Alcohol or not, it would make no difference to the story the townspeople of Skagway would soon have to tell — one of sorrow and sadness, of missed opportunities and rotten luck. The story would revolve around the ship that was just then disappearing from view as the snow started to fall, her 353 passengers and crew blissfully unaware of the dangers that lay ahead. Winter had come now to Skagway, and how dark it would be.

CHAPTER THREE
THE *STAR PRINCESS* SETS SAIL

MONDAY, JUNE 19, 1995
ON BOARD *STAR PRINCESS* IN SEWARD, ALASKA

Nearly seventy-seven years after the Canadian Pacific Steamship *Princess Sophia* had set out from Skagway, a larger, much more modern ship was preparing to do the same. On the evening of Thursday, June 22, 1995, Princess Cruises' *Star Princess* was just pulling in the last of her lines after a successful visit to the famous gold rush town. Her bow lines splashed into the water and were hauled up along the side of her hull, dripping water into the harbour as they went. *Star Princess* was a little over a month into her Alaskan cruise season, which would last until September of that year. For many of her guests the week-long voyage from Seward to Vancouver was a once-in-a-lifetime experience; an escape from the everyday. However, for the crew of the *Star Princess* this southbound voyage was normal and routine. It wasn't an escape from the everyday; it *was* the everyday.

Built in 1988 for Sitmar Cruises as their *FairMajesty*, *Star Princess* would never actually sail for them. Sitmar was put up for sale following the death of the company's founder, Boris Vlasov, in November 1987. Princess Cruises' parent company P&O Cruises snapped up Sitmar in July 1988, and had officially acquired all of their ships — including the still-unfinished *FairMajesty* — by September 1 of that year. *FairMajesty* was renamed *Star Princess* and was formally christened by actress Audrey Hepburn in Miami on March 23, 1989.

High-profile actresses like Hepburn weren't typically known for christening cruise ships at the time, and the news that Hepburn not only performed the traditional ceremonial blessing and the breaking of champagne against the hull, but also spent a week on board her maiden voyage as she sailed around the Caribbean, put *Star Princess* in the public consciousness. Even better for *Princess*, she proved to be a popular and commercially successful ship. While she would operate a variety of voyages over the next six years, *Princess* typically had her winter in the Caribbean and spent her summers cruising the photogenic waters of Alaska.

The voyage had begun innocuously enough. On Monday, June 19, 1995, the 810-foot *Star Princess* came alongside in the small town of Seward, Alaska. Named after Secretary of State William H. Seward, who negotiated the purchase of Alaska from Russia, the town of 3,000 inhabitants served as Princess's northern "turnaround" port on their Alaskan voyages. After a weeklong "northbound" journey from Vancouver, passengers would be disembarked and the ship cleaned and made ready to embark the next set of guests that afternoon. They would spend a week on board as *Star Princess* sailed her third southbound voyage of the season, with an itinerary that called on Prince William Sound, Glacier Bay, Skagway, Juneau, and Ketchikan before their scheduled arrival in Vancouver on Monday, June 26.

Throughout the afternoon, passengers continued to embark the ship. Many had been on pre-cruise land trips that had taken them through Alaska's beautiful Denali National Park, while other guests had chosen to fly in to Anchorage on the day of the sailing. They would be making the long journey from Anchorage International Airport to the piers in Seward, roughly two and a half hours by car. By late evening they would all be on board, settling into their staterooms and ambling up to the pool deck for a cocktail to toast the "midnight sun," which wouldn't set until 11:42 p.m.

By 8:00 p.m. 1,568 passengers were on board. On this voyage *Star Princess* carried with her 639 crew members, for a grand total of 2,207 souls on board. It was a relatively good passenger complement; full double-occupancy was 1,621 guests, meaning only a few staterooms would be sailing empty on the voyage south to Vancouver. That was good news for Princess; they would be making money on this voyage.

The captain of the *Star Princess* held the mandatory lifeboat drill for all those on board. At fifty-four years of age in 1995, Captain Emanuele Chiesa had been at sea for over thirty years, and held both unlimited Italian and Liberian master's licences — essentially the golden ticket on the path for mariners looking to obtain their own command. But while Captain Chiesa oversaw all aspects of the *Star Princess*'s every being during the lifeboat drill, many of the navigational choices while in Alaskan waters had to be deferred to two very important individuals, both of whom were already on board.

Because the itinerary operated by *Star Princess* would remain exclusively in Alaska until after the ship departed Ketchikan for the Canadian waters off the coast of British Columbia, two Southeast Alaska Pilots Association marine pilots would share navigational duties while the *Star Princess* remained in waters designated as compulsory pilotage. They were there to assist the captain and his officers by offering up localized knowledge and expertise to ensure the safe navigation of the vessel in Alaskan waters.

Pilot Ronald Kutz began his maritime career in the 1940s on tugboats, before graduating to the criss-crossing ferry network in Puget Sound and the San Juan Islands aboard the forest-green ships of Washington State Ferries.[1] In 1962 he took the next logical step and graduated to the role of master with the Alaska Marine Highway System; a network of ferries sailing year-round between Alaskan ports, British Columbia, and Washington State. Covering over 5,000 miles of routes and ports between Bellingham, Washington, and Dutch Harbor, Unalaska, it is one of the largest ferry networks in the world. Kutz was also fortunate to have gotten in on the ground floor of the newly formed ferry company, landing a plum appointment as master of the *Taku* before graduating to the *Wikersham* and the *Columbia* in 1974. Kutz spent the next twenty-four years of his life sailing through the often-treacherous waters of Alaska, finally becoming a marine pilot with the Southeast Alaska Marine Pilots Association upon his retirement from the Alaska Marine Highway System in 1987.

Pilot Kutz hadn't been aboard the *Star Princess* in four years, but it didn't take him long to reacquaint himself with the ship's navigation bridge. Like most cruise ships built in the late 1980s, the bridge of the *Star Princess* was comprised of an enclosed wheelhouse containing the ship's main communications and manoeuvring consoles clustered around the forward-facing windows that look out over the ship's bow. Slightly behind them were two additional consoles. The first was a safety console, displaying information relating to the ship's watertight doorways, electrical systems, smoke detectors, and fire doors. The safety console was located on the port, or left, side of the bridge. The second console was located on the starboard, or right, side that consisted of a navigation table where charts showing the exact routes and waypoints of the *Star Princess* were placed. Pencils weren't far from reach — and neither was a hot cup of coffee; the navigator's secret weapon. An auto-pilot computer was placed on the left side of this navigation table, with an additional radar screen to the right of it.

On either side of the enclosed wheelhouse were the ship's bridge wings. Exposed to the elements, they were separated from the wheelhouse by a sliding wooden door that could be latched open or shut as needed. Extending out over the side of the ship, each wing had a console containing all the necessary rudder and propulsion controls to manoeuvre the ship. While the bridge wing isn't commonly used to navigate unless a ship is coming into or going out of port, lookouts can be stationed on either wing to better see what lies ahead.

Five days earlier, just before five in the morning, Pilot Kutz had jumped from the pilot boat through the open shell door of the *Star Princess* as she neared the Point McCartey Pilot Station near Ketchikan. He was beginning a multi-week stint on board with a colleague who had joined the ship in Ketchikan. But Kutz's colleague would only be on board for a few more days. In just two days' time, on June 21, 1995, Pilot Kutz would be paired with a new colleague who would help him guide *Star Princess* on her journey through Lynn Canal. That decision would have significant consequences.

––––––––––

THURSDAY, JUNE 22, 1995
SKAGWAY, ALASKA

Fifty-seven-year-old Alaska State Pilot Robert K. Nerup was a captain in his own right. Beginning his career in the United States Navy in 1956, Nerup served in active duty at sea for nearly two decades. By the time he retired from the navy in 1980 he was a commanding officer aboard a tugboat. He went on to a civilian career as a marine pilot, joining the Southeast Alaska Marine Pilots Association. His qualifications didn't end there. Nerup also held a U.S. Coast Guard master's licence that he had just renewed the previous January, and an Alaska State Pilot's licence that he renewed in December of 1994.[2]

Just the day before, June 21, at quarter to eleven in the morning, Pilot Nerup had boarded the *Star Princess* as she cruised through Glacier Bay, Alaska. While her guests were on-deck admiring the splendour of their surroundings and waiting with baited breath for their first glimpse of the towering face of Margerie Glacier, Pilot Nerup made his way through the myriad of corridors and public rooms up to the ship's navigation bridge. There he met his colleague and fellow pilot, Ronald Kutz.

Having been on board for several days already, Kutz brought Nerup up to speed on what had, up to that point, been a rather uneventful voyage. Both men agreed that it would be prudent to split their shifts evenly down the middle for the remainder of the voyage, with a six-hour-on, six-hour-off rotating schedule. Pilot Nerup got to work immediately, taking the 12:30 to 18:30 shift, followed by the 00:30 to 06:30 watch. Pilot Kutz would handle the hours between 18:30 and 00:30, and 06:30 to 12:30 — as he had for his entire duration on board.

During this brief introduction period, Pilot Nerup also met Captain Emanuele Chiesa. At least, he should have. Captain Chiesa would later testify that he and Nerup talked about what would "happen" during the voyage; a vague description that probably entailed going over arrival and departure times and other crucial navigation concerns. Robert Nerup, however, would later claim the meeting had never taken place.

Like most men who have lived for nearly six decades on this planet, Nerup was not without his faults. For the previous eight years he had been treated for depression; an affliction that had snuck up on the experienced pilot in his late forties. It wasn't entirely without cause, either. For

Nerup, 1987 had been a disastrous year, which he would likely rather forget.

His problems had begun on March 21, 1987, when a small vessel he was piloting collided with a log raft in Hobart Bay, just north of Petersburg. A little over a month later, on April 28, Hobart Bay would once again play a crucial role in Robert Nerup's life, as another vessel under his pilotage ran aground there.

The knock-on effect of these two accidents was a defining moment for Nerup. Prohibited from piloting a vessel in the state of Alaska until 1989, he was required to attend additional training and skills classes in order to reinstate his licence. He fulfilled all the requirements and was granted his licence. He returned to the waters of Alaska ever so briefly, from 1989 to 1990. But trouble had a way of finding Robert Nerup. Just two years after having his marine pilot's licence reinstated, he was involved in another, much higher profile, accident involving a ship under his command.

On May 27, 1991, just before seven o'clock in the morning, Nerup was piloting Princess Cruises' 553-foot *Island Princess* as she came into Skagway Bay. Except for the strong winds racing down Lynn Canal — which weren't so unusual — it was shaping up to be a brilliant morning. Not a trace of cloud could be seen in the sky and plenty of sunshine was already bathing the ship's open decks.

At the same time that the *Island Princess* was gliding along the sunlit sea, Regency Cruises' *Regent Sea* was also steaming slowly across Skagway Bay. At 631 feet in length, the rugged ex-ocean liner had nearly one hundred feet of length on the *Island Princess*. But having been built in 1957, and lacking the built-in thruster propulsion added to the bows of newer ships, she was being guided into port with the assistance of a tug boat. The *Island Princess*, built in 1971, was able to manoeuvre into port on her own thanks to a bow thruster that made lateral movements possible.

Without warning, everything went haywire. "We saw curtains and sparks and a puff of smoke. We didn't know what the hell happened," passenger Lynn Biller would later tell the Associated Press.[3] Biller was standing at the stern of the *Regent Sea* when the *Island Princess* seemingly drifted straight toward their ship. Instead of stopping, both ships remained on a collision course, and passengers standing at the rail braced themselves for impact. When the two vessels finally hit, the force of the collision ripped the steel hull plating from the *Regent Sea* and tore a fifty-foot gash in the side of the *Island Princess*. Located thirty feet or so above the waterline, the tear literally ripped the outer steel hull from eleven staterooms, exposing them to the elements. Three of the six hundred passengers aboard *Island Princess* suffered minor injuries from broken glass, while no injuries were reported on the larger *Regent Sea*.

Of the two ships in Skagway Bay that morning, the *Island Princess* bore the brunt of the accident. Although her structure and sea-keeping abilities weren't affected by the collision, the loss of eleven staterooms during the start of the Alaska cruise season ensured that she would have to go into dry dock for repairs. After both Princess Cruises and the Coast Guard had assessed the situation, the *Island Princess* sailed from Skagway bound for the Todd Shipyards in Seattle. Her passengers — and Pilot Nerup — were not on board for the journey.[4]

Regency Cruises fared far better. The accident didn't impact the *Regent Sea*'s schedule, and repairs were made to her bent stern plating and railings as she was underway in Lynn Canal, en route to Juneau. While Regency Cruises stated in a press release that "The minor damage sustained to an aft section of the *Regent Sea*'s mooring deck [did] not affect passenger facilities nor the ship's structural integrity," the event did make the news.[5] Once again, Robert Nerup found himself without a licence to act as a marine pilot; this time for a duration of six months, effectively ending his Alaska cruise pilotage season before it had even begun.

In order to have his licence reinstated, Nerup was required to complete a one-day course in shipboard radar, coupled with a two-week course on ship handling and navigation — including tests on "navigation management," a term for how members of the ship's crew interact with each other when on duty on the bridge. Nerup would also be forced to take another test governing the "rules of the road" at sea, and would remain on probation for a full year after that.

For every one of the requirements that the State of Alaska and the Transportation Safety Board had set forth for him, Robert Nerup fulfilled each. With his courses once again passed and his licence reinstated, he returned to piloting cruise ships in Alaska in the spring of 1993. But the accidents had left him shaken.

To combat his long-standing depression, he had been taking Effexor at 18:00 each evening since 1992. The antidepressant seems to have alleviated the worst of his symptoms, leaving Pilot Nerup with only a handful of physical side effects that he was able to easily deal with.

Juneau, Alaska, appears today much as it did in 1918. Ships still dock here, though they bring mainly travellers taking an Alaska cruise vacation.

As he ate his dinner on the evening of June 22, 1995, while *Star Princess* was still docked in Skagway, Nerup took his daily dose of the drug. He hadn't told anyone that he was taking Effexor, and no one — including the Southeast Alaska Marine Pilots Association — ever thought to ask. He rubbed his eyes and looked out at the imposing mountains surrounding the ship. He hadn't slept well during the past twenty-four hours, partly due to the demands of the job and partly because of the altered scheduling for this next leg of the cruise.

The railroad dock in Skagway, shown here in September 1949. The docks were configured so that trains could pull up on the full length of the pier, thus avoiding the need to walk from the main WP&YR station, which was situated at the end of Broadway. Although heavily modernized, this docking location is still used by cruise ships.

Pilots Kutz and Nerup had decided that for the run from Skagway to Juneau through Lynn Canal they would modify their six-on, six-off schedule to better accommodate the shorter length of the journey. Both men agreed to stand watch for five hours and fifteen minutes apiece, with Pilot Kutz overseeing the 19:00 hrs departure of *Star Princess* from Skagway. Pilot Nerup would be officially on duty at forty minutes past midnight on the morning of June 23, 1995.

Because *Star Princess* had been docked for much of the day, the services of both pilots hadn't been needed. Hypothetically, this should have been a day of rest for both men, but sleep wasn't coming easily to Pilot Nerup.

That day he had stood watch from 00:30 until the *Star Princess* came alongside in Skagway at 06:00, at which point he retired to his stateroom to sleep. He awoke at noon, ate lunch, and remained awake until 14:00 that afternoon before returning to his stateroom. Nerup then managed to get three more hours of shut-eye before awaking at 17:00 to have dinner and take his Effexor. By the time he finished dinner and finally crawled back into his bunk at 19:00, Robert Nerup had woken up and gone to sleep four separate times in less than twenty-four hours.

This lack of sleep likely didn't give Nerup cause for concern; after all, he knew *Star Princess* inside and out, having last joined her for a two-week stint on May 17 as she began her Alaska season. This was just one of ten trips Nerup had made aboard the ship in the past few years — more than enough to know how she responded to helm commands and handled at various speeds.

Alaska marine pilots aren't exclusive to any one ship or cruise line, but it speaks to Nerup's character that so much of his work involved the ships of Princess Cruises, even after the collision on board the *Island Princess* three years previously. If the line had any misgivings about his presence on board their ships, they certainly didn't express them publicly.

As the engines of the *Star Princess* rumbled to life, Captain Chiesa deftly guided his ship away from Skagway's railroad dock and out into the open expanse of Lynn Canal. Her screws bit into the churning water, whipped up by Skagway's trademark wind, as she came around to port. Being the middle of summer, passengers gathered on the open decks to admire this scenic departure. In the distance, the White Pass & Yukon Route trains slowly pulled away from the railroad dock, their work hauling tourists to the summit and back done for another day.

Once the *Star Princess* was clear of the harbour and well on her way, Captain Chiesa gave control of his ship to Pilot Ronald Kutz. It was a little after seven thirty in the evening. In roughly five hours he would pass the torch to Pilot Nerup, who would guide the vessel the remainder of the way to Juneau.

Their routine voyage was about to change dramatically.

CHAPTER FOUR
THE STORM
— PRINCESS SOPHIA

THURSDAY, OCTOBER 24, 1918
TRANSITING LYNN CANAL, ALASKA
ABOARD *PRINCESS SOPHIA*

Like most great disasters, the seeds of this one were sewn innocuously. As the ship's clocks on board the *Princess Sophia* hit midnight and the date silently slipped over into the first seconds of Thursday, October 24, 1918, the men who stood on her navigation bridge were facing a series of minor annoyances.

First, there was her late departure from Skagway — three hours in total — that would put *Princess Sophia* behind schedule for the remainder of her journey south unless they could make up time. Making up time, however, was beginning to look impossible: less than an hour after setting sail from Skagway a raging snowstorm kicked up as they passed the small town of Haines, Alaska, and entered into the widest stretch of Lynn Canal. Captain Leonard Locke, a stickler for adhering to published schedule times, kept her speed up in the hopes of making up time. With the fierce snow came winds that were bearing down from the north, hitting the *Princess Sophia* at her stern with gusts of up to fifty miles per hour. The high

winds also kicked up heavy swells, and *Princess Sophia* began to pitch and roll heavily as she drove on through the growing storm, bound for Juneau.

The nasty, hard-driving winter storm would surely result in an uncomfortable ride for the 278 passengers, but it was far from the worst storm that the men on the bridge that night had ever seen. Along with Captain Locke, First Officer Jerry Shaw strained to see much beyond the foredeck mast. Although all of the lights before the bridge and in the wheelhouse had been extinguished prior to setting sail from Skagway, *Princess Sophia*'s running and navigation lights were now acting as miniature spotlights against the snow, illuminating each flake as if it were a high-intensity light bulb as it zipped past.

At age thirty-six, First Officer Shaw was half as old as Captain Locke. He also took home half the pay — roughly $160 per month compared with Locke's relative haul of $300. He'd been with Canadian Pacific for twenty years, and was both well-liked and well-respected. The year 1918 hadn't

An officer peers out the window of the *Princess Adelaide*'s wheelhouse. Note the drop-down windows; the wheehouse of the *Princess Sophia* would have been very similar in layout and design.

been the best for the young officer, though. In April, while commanding the 165-foot long Canadian Pacific salvage vessel *Tees*, Shaw found himself caught up in rapidly changing currents near Sidney, British Columbia, just southeast of the provincial capital of Victoria. Making twelve knots at the time, the small *Tees* was rapidly pushed off-course by the fast-moving water.[1] Before Shaw or the other officers on her bridge could react, she ran aground on a submerged reef near Zero Point. Both passengers and mail were successfully taken off, and the *Tees* was pumped out and towed into port. The experience, however, clearly rattled Shaw. As he would later tell the *Victoria Daily Colonist* newspaper, the entire event "was entirely unexpected."[2]

Satisfied that the accident was unavoidable, Canadian Pacific put their trust in Shaw again. This was his second trip on the *Princess Sophia*, and his last run south before being transferred to another vessel for the winter months. The events of April aboard the *Tees*, however, were not lost on Shaw as he watched the weather outside the warm wheelhouse turn increasingly nasty. He glanced over at Locke, who stared straight ahead into the darkness. The experienced sea captain didn't seem ruffled in the least by the weather. *Princess Sophia* continued to steam south at twelve knots, her whistles sounding at regular intervals throughout the night.

Several other men joined them in *Princess Sophia*'s increasingly cramped wheelhouse. Canadian Pacific's regulations mandated that in adverse weather no less than two officers would be present on the bridge, and two lookouts were to be stationed. The job of actually steering the ship fell to one of two quartermasters, thirty-three-year-old W.

Evans and twenty-five-year-old W.K. Liggett. History hasn't recorded who was actually at the helm of the *Princess Sophia* that night, but the regular change of watch occurred at midnight. Regardless of which quartermaster came on duty during the blinding snowstorm, he would have been fresh and ready for his four-hour stint from midnight to 4 a.m.

Outside on deck, exposed to the elements, was an eighteen-year-old boy named L. Smith. On this trip south he had the unenviable role of being *Princess Sophia*'s sole lookout. The other lookout scheduled to be on board for the sailing was Walter Gosse — brother of Second Officer Frank Gosse. Prior to departure from Vancouver, the two brothers had attended a dance. Like most young men attending dances with pretty girls, they'd pushed their exit from the dance floor until the very last second and had to sprint to *Princess Sophia*'s berthing location at Vancouver's Pier D. Frank Gosse made it, but Walter was left standing pierside. The lack of a second lookout was inconvenient but not unsolvable; in all likelihood, Locke and Shaw had stationed an able-bodied seaman out on deck to assist young Lookout Smith.

In the darkness of the wheelhouse an oversized poster was mounted to one of the bulkheads. Under the direction of Canadian Pacific's British Columbia manager, Captain James Troupe, every vessel in the coastal fleet was fitted with such a poster in the wheelhouse. It detailed "right-of-way" rules for passing vessels within the coastal waterway system. Troup had reasoned that, if in doubt, officers could quickly and easily consult the chart without having to go to the chart room and look through booklets filled with information, thus wasting valuable and perhaps precious time.

Vancouver harbour as it would have appeared in 1918.

Located at the foot of Granville Street, Vancouver's Pier D is shown here in 1914. It would burn to the ground in a spectacular fire on July 27, 1938.

City of Vancouver Archives AM358-S1-: CVA 152-1.097

The chart room aboard *Princess Sophia* held the vast majority of information sources that the officer of the watch would likely need. Buried in amongst the papers and booklets that filled this room were two directives from Canadian Pacific headquarters to all captains. The first of these notices was over three years old, dated August 12, 1915:

To ALL Masters and Officers:
Now that the foggy season is approaching, I must

caution you regarding the necessity of extreme care in the navigation of your ship in thick weather. Strict attention must be paid to the Company's printed Rules and International Rules of the Road regarding safe navigation.

Neglect to carry out the caution — "Stop the Engines" — contained in the second paragraph of Article #16, will not be excused.

Remember that the responsibilities for the protection of life and property under your charge are very great, and that the strictest observation of Rules and Regulations laid down, are the best safeguards for your passengers, the Company, and yourself.

OBEY THE RULES. TAKE NO CHANCES.

APPROVED: J.W. Troup, Manager. C.D. NEROUTSOS. Marine Superintendent.[3]

The second directive was less than a year old. It was issued on November 20, 1917, and said mainly the same thing as the 1915 missive, with one important addition: "Remember that at the present time it is practically impossible to replace a vessel, and that all repairs cost from two to three times what they did before the war."[4]

The message was clear: masters were to avoid accidents and incidents at all cost.

Princess Sophia's whistles cut through the midnight blizzard again, rattling the decking as they sounded. The deep-throated sound reverberated off the high mountain faces surrounding the ship. Viewed from above, she was but a brightly lit speck travelling alone down one of Alaska's most dangerous stretches of water. Although she continued to steam south at twelve knots, with three men in her wheelhouse and two lookouts positioned on deck, she was literally feeling her way through.

Despite the foul weather directives from the company — which he surely must have seen and no doubt remembered — Captain Locke was unperturbed by the storm that greeted him in the early morning hours of Thursday, October 24. As he had on past voyages, the experienced sea captain was planning to take a mostly straight course through Lynn Canal from Eldred Rock to Point Sherman. Once he was one and a half miles off Point Sherman, he would plot a straight course past Sentinel Island that would take him between Sentinel Island and Vanderbilt Reef. Even with the relatively modern conveyances of 1918, successfully navigating Lynn Canal was still as touch and go as the earliest days of sail.

Running for more than 140 kilometres between the Chilkat River north of Skagway to Chatham Strait and Stephen's Passage near Juneau, Lynn Canal's chief claim to fame is being North America's deepest fjord. Beneath the churning surface lies 610 metres of water, all of which is guarded by a series of immense mountain ranges that seemingly rise straight out of the depths. During the daytime it's a gorgeous sight, and in the twenty years since the gold rush, navigation here had improved significantly. In November 1887 J. Bernard Moore, one of the founding settlers of Skagway, left the small settlement that was then known as Mooresville and sailed south for the winter. He didn't get far — within hours his small ship ran into the same kind of weather that was now bearing down on the *Princess Sophia*, and he was forced to turn back. After nearly six days of dodging storms and seeking shelter in anchorages tucked into the mountains, he successfully reached Juneau.[5] Three decades later, *Princess Sophia* could perform the same feat, in the same fearsome weather, in a matter of hours.

As southbound ships neared Juneau the workload on their masters and officers increased exponentially. Instead of the north end's relatively comfortable width of eight to ten miles, the southern end of Lynn Canal is a maze of islands, reefs, and obstacles with a shipping lane that at the time was not much more than three miles across. After southbound ships passed Berners Bay to the east and entered the aptly named Favorite Channel in order to reach Juneau, they're met with a triple threat to the west: Lincoln Island, Shelter Island, and Lena Point.

Before ships reach any of these islands, however, there are two more obstacles to face as Lynn Canal is traded for Favorite Channel: the frequently submerged rocky outcrop that is Vanderbilt Reef and its smaller cousin to the south, Poundstone Rock.

Vanderbilt Reef was named not for the famous Vanderbilt family, but for J.M Vanderbilt, who had discovered it five years prior while acting as master of a small vessel doing survey and mapping work on behalf of the United States Navy. When his ship, the *Favorite*, came across the reef, Captain Vanderbilt determined that it was spread across the surface of the water for about half an acre. More troubling, he found it was nearly completely covered at high tide, and regularly obscured altogether if inclement weather produced large swells that helped to mask its rocky shores. At the most extreme low tide, in calm seas, approximately twelve feet of Vanderbilt reef would poke above the surface of the water.[6] Maps were drawn up, and the reef was eventually named for Vanderbilt by a fellow captain, Lester Anthony Beardslee, who spent many years in Alaskan waters as commander of the USS *Jamestown*.

Canadian Pacific had, like many shipping lines, tried to petition the American government to place a warning light on Vanderbilt Reef. Their most recent attempt, in 1917, had not brought about any substantial change. The Americans determined that with the Great War still raging on in Europe, putting a warning light on Vanderbilt Reef was simply uneconomical. Steamship traffic through Lynn Canal wasn't what it had been during the gold rush twenty years earlier, and there were more high-priority locations in Alaska deserving of lighthouses and warning lights. As a concession, a small buoy was installed, anchored on a submerged ridge of the reef. In bad weather, the buoy was frequently obscured by heavy seas. At night it couldn't be seen at all.

Even during daylight hours, the navigational aid on Vanderbilt Reef turned out to be a meaningless concession. Most mariners sailing Lynn Canal had been doing so, completely unaided, since the days of the gold rush. A few had even sailed these waters prior to 1897, when no one except for a few lone prospectors had any real interest in travelling here.

Given the heavy seas, high winds, and driving snow that night, it's highly unlikely that any of the men in the wheelhouse of the *Princess Sophia* were actively looking for the Vanderbilt Reef buoy. With the ship pitching and rolling with the heavy seas and the heavy snow and high winds obscuring visibility, their focus was likely concentrated on finding the safest route through the storm to Juneau.

The Canadian Pacific steamship *Princess May* aground on Sentinel Island on August 5, 1910. All passengers and crew were rescued, and the ship was eventually salvaged.

Poundstone Rock, on the other hand, lies in a most inconvenient place, nearly dead centre in the entrance to Favorite Channel. When only one ship is passing toward Juneau, with Poundstone Rock to their port side, it presents no navigational challenge. If two vessels are approaching at the same time, the margin for error narrows considerably.

That danger was not lost on the men on the bridge of the *Princess Sophia* that night. Just a few years earlier, in August

1910, the Canadian Pacific steamer *Princess May* was sailing these very waters when she ran into trouble. Departing from Skagway with eighty passengers, sixty-six crew members, and a hold full of gold, she was heading on a southerly course through Lynn Canal. Instead of a snowstorm obscuring the view of her officers, it was a thick, soup-like fog that impeded their ability to see ahead of their ship that night. By the time they realized they were headed for Sentinel Island, it was too late to stop the massive ship. At a speed of ten knots, she drove bow-first into Sentinel Island. The force of the collision, coupled with the forward momentum of the enormously heavy vessel, drove her up onto the rocks, where she sat at a peculiar angle, bows high in the air, screws completely out of the water. It was as if she was on some magnificent sloping dry dock that was slowly sinking stern-first into the sea.

Complicating matters was the fact that the ship had the latest in wireless technology, but it was completely dependent on the vessel's dynamos that provided electrical power to the ship; no battery backup had been installed. Wireless operator W.R. Keller had just enough time to tap out a single message, but it was a powerful one that saved the lives of those on board:

S.S. PRINCESS MAY SINKING SENTINEL ISLAND; SEND HELP[7]

While all those aboard the *Princess May* had been successfully rescued, Canadian Pacific was less than pleased with the damage inflicted to their ship. Refloated in September 1910, repairs to the *Princess May* would continue until the spring of 1911, when she finally resumed service. In all, one hundred twenty steel hull plates had to be completely replaced. The largest hole in the ship's hull had measured over fifty feet in length, and was just one of dozens that had to be repaired before the ship could sail again. The cost to Canadian Pacific was enormous for the time: $115,000 U.S. dollars, plus the cost of compensation to her passengers and the revenue lost while she was out of service.

Eight years later, the men on the bridge of the *Princess Sophia* are eager to avoid a repeat of that career-ending performance.

Princess Sophia's whistles sounded again. The snowstorm had lent the night skies a surrealistic orange hue, and increasingly large snowflakes continued to whip past the curved windows of the wheelhouse. Captain Locke and First Officer Shaw stood on opposite sides of the wheelhouse, quietly looking into the darkness. Except for the howling of the wind and the creaking of the ship as she drove through the night, the two men remained silent for the most part. The odd exception was made for commands given to the quartermaster, who would repeat each command as it was given and then confirm to the two senior officers once the ship had reached her desired heading.

Both men were acutely aware that they would soon pass Point Sherman. Once they were there, Locke could take a compass reading to determine the exact course that would allow him to pass between Vanderbilt Reef and Sentinel Island. That is, if he could see the point. With the snow still obscuring visibility, he used an old mariner's trick. He ordered *Princess Sophia*'s whistle to be sounded once again. As it cried out into the darkness, the old sea captain slowly shifted his weight from his left foot to his right and back again. Quietly, under his breath, he began to count: One thousand and one. One thousand and two …

The grounding of the *Tees* would weigh heavily on First Officer Jerry Shaw, who was eager to avoid a repeat of that accident the night *Princess Sophia* sailed from Skagway.

Locke waited for the echoes from the ship's whistle to reverberate back from the high mountain peaks of Lynn Canal. When they finally returned, he could gauge — more or less — where she was in relation to the canal itself.[8] Noting the ship's position, he had either First Officer Shaw or the quartermaster sound the ship's whistles again. Again, he shifted his feet. "One thousand and one. One thousand and two …"

Satisfied with his findings, Locke now ordered a change in course. *Princess Sophia* began slowly swinging around to port, lining up on a heading that the men on the bridge believed would lead them safely into Favorite Channel and on to Juneau. First Officer Shaw entered the time and heading into the ship's log book. It was a little after two in the morning on October 24, 1918.

Exactly what happened in the wheelhouse during those lonely hours after departure from Skagway remains unknown. The thick log books kept in the chart room aboard the *Princess Sophia* that recorded every change of watch, every course correction, and every anomaly encountered on the journey south were headed for the same fate as her passengers, crew, and cargo. What is known is that the officers on watch that night were certainly not lacking in experience. They drew on that experience to navigate through Lynn Canal just as they always had in inclement weather. If Captain Locke was overconfident in his abilities, it's reasonable to assume First Officer Shaw's shakeup in April on board the *Tees* made him wary of what he could not physically see. He would have been aware of every perceived increase or decrease in the severity of the weather, sensitive to every wayward creak and groan in the ship's superstructure. He probably hovered near the ship's compass, taking whatever readings he could.

The real question, though, is whether First Officer Shaw — at half the age, half the rank, and half the pay of his commanding officer — had the courage to pass along any doubts he had that evening to the higher-ranking, more experienced Captain Locke.

In most maritime accidents there is a striking moment of clarity, just before trouble is encountered. The crew of the RMS *Titanic* experienced this on the evening of April 14, 1912, when they had only seconds to identify the iceberg that lay directly in their path. Orders were given: the ship's helm was put "hard-a-starboard" and the engine telegraphs forcefully rung to signal "Full Astern."

Aboard the RMS *Lusitania* in 1915 fog had prevented the officers on her bridge from seeing much of anything on the morning of May 7th. By the time lunch was underway in the ship's dining room, the fog had been replaced by a brilliant, sunny afternoon. That sunshine allowed a lookout stationed on the bow to see the wake of a torpedo racing through the water. It took only seconds to reach the ship, but in those few moments clarity came through with surprising force.

Princess Sophia's whistles rang out through the night again — and this time they echoed back differently. The report was burbled, garbled somehow. The time was ten minutes after two in the morning. History doesn't record who saw it first, or if anyone saw it at all. Chances are if someone did it was one of the lookouts stationed out on deck. Cold, stamping their feet and breathing into their hands to keep warm, they probably glimpsed it ever so briefly. It looked like a shadow to begin with — a bit of nothing in the water. The shadow had depth to it, though. Could it be a wave? Someone went over to the railing to look at it, but as quickly as it had revealed itself it seemed to have disappeared again, lost in a mass of snow and heavy seas. Eyes squinted, peering into the darkness. Straining. Searching. Something was off.

It's not difficult to imagine the snowstorm letting up — just for a second. Just long enough for clarity to slam into the two lookouts on deck. Captain Locke probably saw it, too, along with First Officer Jerry Shaw. At his station set back from the wheelhouse windows, and with dozens of feet of bow in front of him, the quartermaster on duty likely remained blissfully unaware that *Princess Sophia* was headed straight for Vanderbilt Reef.

No one remembers hearing the ship's propulsion suddenly grow louder, or vibrate with a sudden change in direction. There were no alarms, no bells, and no metal clanging that might have foreshadowed what was to come. If they saw Vanderbilt Reef lying in their path, no one on the bridge that night had time to react.

In seconds, fate would come to call on the *Princess Sophia*. For her passengers and crew, however, the ordeal was just beginning.

Even in the middle of June, fog can roll in unexpectedly in Alaska. This modern photograph, taken near Sitka, shows how fog can completely obliterate the landscape. A similar situation faced the would-be rescuers who struggled to reach the wreck of the *Princess Sophia* in the days before radar navigation.

At ten minutes past two in the morning, on Thursday, October 24, 1918, the 245-foot *Princess Sophia* crashed head-on into Vanderbilt Reef. She was making between eleven and twelve knots at the time, and her twin screws thrashed violently at the water around them as her long, slender bow rose out of the water. Driven forward by the still-turning propellers, her bow ripped and scraped its way along the sharp reef, popping rivets and crunching the lowest plates of her hull and keel as if they were made of tin.

CHAPTER FIVE
THE TURN
– STAR PRINCESS

MIDNIGHT, JUNE 23, 1995
ON BOARD *STAR PRINCESS*

Separated by nearly eight decades from the *Princess Sophia*, Princess Cruises' *Star Princess* was nevertheless making her way down the same stretch of water. After their departure from Skagway on the evening of June 22, 1995, the massive vessel had entered into Lynn Canal proper and was beginning the relatively short journey down to Juneau.

The weather for their overnight cruising was generally quite good. Except for some moderately strong winds coming at them from the south and overcast skies, it was a nice evening to be sailing in Lynn Canal.

Second Officer Gampiero Landi peered into the growing darkness and let his eyes slowly adjust to the light that was, at long last, slowly fading. Officially, the sun had set at 10:08 p.m., but this far north in the middle of June, twilight lasted for hours. If anything, it was slightly darker than usual out, thanks to the partly cloudy skies that sheltered much of the ambient light, but Landi knew the sun would be back up in about three hours. *Star Princess* was making an easy ten knots as she sailed toward Juneau, the halfway point of her seven-night Alaska cruise from Vancouver.

Landi was in the first minutes of his watch rotation, which would last until four in the morning, and he had already run into problems. At their current speed of ten knots, Landi calculated that *Star Princess* was going to arrive in Juneau much sooner than she had been scheduled for — and that presented the experienced mariner with a logistical problem. Longshoremen had already been contracted to be on the pier in Juneau at 05:15 to receive the first lines from *Star Princess*, but Landi figured they were going to arrive much sooner than that; possibly as early as 03:45. An early arrival would throw everything off, and force *Star Princess* to anchor in Gastineau Channel for well over an hour and a half.

As the senior officer on watch aboard the *Star Princess* in the early morning hours of June 23, 1995, their unexpectedly early arrival became Landi's overriding problem.

Assisting Second Officer Landi with the ship's navigational operation was Third Officer Vincenzo Alcaras. At twenty-nine years of age, he'd been at sea since 1986 and had been employed by Princess since November 1990. This was his second season in Alaska, and he'd spent about seven months serving aboard the *Star Princess*. He knew the ship well, and had even met Pilot Nerup before, on his first season in Alaska back in 1993. That night his primary task was helping Second Officer Landi to monitor the pilot's navigational choices and plotting the ship's position on the navigational charts for the voyage. He had never met Pilot Ronald Kutz before.

Also located on the bridge — albeit further afar — was Quartermaster Hilmi Masdar, who at age thirty-one had been an able-bodied seaman for more than half his life. He'd been with Princess Cruises since 1991, but that night he had the unenviable task of acting as lookout on the port-side bridge wing, which was open and exposed to the force 3 winds that were racing along the channel toward the *Star Princess* at a speed of ten knots. Even though it was the beginning of summer, the chilled air still nipped at Quartermaster Masdar, who shifted back and forth on his feet in an effort to keep warm.

At the ship's helm, back inside the enclosed wheelhouse, was Quartermaster Basri Hasan, a forty-seven-year-old seaman who had been with Princess since December 1991. He was responsible for turning the ship when one of the officers or the pilot called out a navigational instruction. Each hour on the hour he swapped places with Quartermaster Masdar on the bridge wing to allow his colleague to keep warm.

Not wanting to contend with the unwanted scheduling effects of an early arrival into Juneau, Second Officer Landi strolled over to Pilot Kutz at ten minutes after midnight and told him that the ship was moving too fast. Landi asked Kutz to swing the vessel around in Lynn Canal to burn up some speed and time, a move that Landi had performed — and had seen performed — many times before. At its widest point, Lynn Canal spans nineteen kilometres from side to side; at their current position over eleven kilometres remained, more than enough space to bring the 245-metre *Star Princess* around. Landi reckoned the entire turn should take about thirty minutes to complete, and would put the ship in better shape to arrive in Juneau on time.

Pilot Kutz told Landi that he was leery about performing the mid-channel manoeuvre, and suggested that they simply drop their speed to below eight knots. With the reduction in propulsion power, *Star Princess* should come in closer to her scheduled arrival time.

This was when a brief tug of war occurred between the two men.

On board modern ships an interesting balance of power exists between pilots and the crews of the vessels they're overseeing. Nowhere is this truer than in Alaska, where marine pilots essentially have control over a vessel for the entire duration of its journey due to the unique navigational challenges these waters present. But it also creates a unique double standard whereby pilots have control over the vessel, but the crew — who remain on board for months at a time — know the performance characteristics of their ship better than the pilot.

The senior officer of the watch is responsible for matching up the ship's plotted track with the current position, and for ensuring the navigation orders of the pilot are carried out promptly. If the senior officer of the watch notices something is amiss and the vessel is moving into danger, his duty is to warn the pilot of any navigational or operational hazards that might exist. If the pilot takes no action, watch officers are to notify the master of the vessel.

Second Officer Landi stared out the windows of the navigation bridge and considered the proposal. Turning to Ronald Kutz, he told the experienced pilot that he was reluctant to drop the speed of the *Star Princess* below eight knots because he felt the ship's performance began to seriously degrade at that speed. The 810-foot-long ship did not steer well at very low speeds, and Landi wanted to keep his options open in the event an emergency manoeuvre was required. Instead, he again recommended that Pilot Kutz simply bring *Star Princess* around in a "slow starboard swing" that would backtrack around on their current position before rejoining their previously plotted course. With no traffic in the canal, Second Officer Landi's idea seems like a safe and ideal solution that would allow them to arrive in Juneau later while keeping the vessel's speed up, in case anything should arise.

As odd as it may sound, turning ships around in Lynn Canal isn't that uncommon. When other marine traffic isn't present, the manoeuvre represents little to no danger to a ship. In fact, the only real notification provided by Princess on the line's Nav.7.2. Pilotage Information Card about swinging a vessel around in pilotage waters reads: "When a ship is being swung in pilotage waters, the position must be monitored throughout the swing by radar ranges and/or clearing bearings or angles." [1]

Pilot Kutz once again voiced his preference to simply drop *Star Princess*'s speed to below eight knots, but Second Officer Landi put his foot down and quashed the idea. He ordered Kutz to make the turn.

The two men weren't unhappy with each other; far from it. Pilot Kutz was just as happy to make the turn as he was to slow the ship's speed, but completing the turn required an increased amount of work and vigilance from the entire navigation team on the darkened bridge of the *Star Princess*. While Kutz still felt that decreasing the speed of *Star Princess* was the best option, he honoured the wishes of Second Officer Landi and told Quartermaster Basri Hasan, who had been at the helm the entire time, to bring the vessel around to starboard using a maximum turn of five degrees right rudder. Quartermaster Hasan complied, moving the ship's wheel over to the right. In the channel, the massive *Star Princess* began to slowly swing around to starboard. The clock on the bridge read fifteen minutes past midnight.

Halfway into the turn, at 00:30, Pilot Kutz requested that Pilot Nerup be awakened to relieve him. Kutz's five-hour stint on the bridge was coming to a close, and Nerup would take over piloting duties from him until the vessel reached Juneau in the morning. The bridge was quiet, except for the occasional beep or clack from the navigation equipment. At 00:40, satisfied that the turn to starboard had been completed successfully, Pilot Kutz had Quartermaster Hasan put *Star Princess* back on a course of 143°T, bound for their navigational waypoint at Sentinel Island Light.

Just as Quartermaster Hasan was bringing the ship back on course, relief Pilot Robert Nerup emerged on the bridge. As is common practice whenever a change of watch is taking place, he and the outgoing Pilot Kutz spent about fifteen minutes together while Nerup let his eyes adjusts to the darkness before the bridge. The two men made small talk and discussed the recently performed manoeuvre, without involving Second Officer Landi. This in itself was not uncommon; at the time, pilots typically didn't share information with the other officers on watch, and the officers on watch didn't typically ask. When he entered the bridge, Robert Nerup's presence wasn't even formally announced to the bridge team, nor was his assumption of command, at forty-five minutes past the hour. It was as if he and Pilot Kutz were one and the same.

Before departing the bridge for the warmth of his own stateroom, Pilot Kutz showed the incoming Nerup their current position. He led him over to the ship's automatic radar piloting aid (ARPA) unit, located on the starboard side of the wheelhouse. Kutz also showed Nerup visually — as best he could in near total darkness — their location physically by looking out of the wheelhouse windows.

Nerup also pointed across the expanse of the bridge to Quartermaster Masdar, who was still acting as lookout on the exposed portside bridge wing.

At 00:55, Pilot Ronald J. Kutz bid his colleague farewell and exited the navigation bridge via the doorway at the aft end of the room, next to the fire control panel. It had been a long day, and Kutz was looking forward to turning in to his comfortable berth on board the *Star Princess* for a few hours of shut-eye.

On the bridge, Second Officer Landi stared into the darkness ahead. Quartermaster Masdar was on the bridge wing. Quartermaster Hasan held the vessel on her current course. With his colleague gone, Pilot Robert Nerup took his eyes off the bridge windows overlooking the bow and adjusted the ARPA radar's twelve-inch view screen to the six-mile scale, offset to provide a larger view of radar coverage in front of the vessel. He bent over in front of its softly glowing screen as the digital clock in the wheelhouse changed from 00:59 to 01:00.

No one noticed that *Star Princess* was actually sailing one mile to the west of her intended track.

CHAPTER SIX
THE ACCIDENT
– PRINCESS SOPHIA

THURSDAY, OCTOBER 24, 1918

ABOARD *PRINCESS SOPHIA* ON VANDERBILT REEF, ALASKA

In the four hours she'd put between her and Skagway, the *Princess Sophia* had managed a rather remarkable feat. Pounded by heavy seas and enveloped by a raging snowstorm that refused to let up, she had nonetheless managed to travel over forty nautical miles through Lynn Canal. That was a respectable distance, which was no doubt aided by the winds that roared into her stern at up to fifty miles per hour.

However, no one noticed she was completely off course.

At ten minutes past two in the morning, on Thursday, October 24, 1918, the 245-foot *Princess Sophia* crashed head on into Vanderbilt Reef. She was making between eleven and twelve knots at the time, and her twin screws thrashed violently at the water around them as her long slender bow rose out of the water. Driven forward by the still-turning propellers, her bow ripped and scraped its way along the sharp reef, popping rivets and crunching the lowest plates of her hull and keel as if they were made of tin. The reef, barely visible above the churning seas, acted as a miniature launch: rather than crumpling her bow and

stopping her dead in her tracks, the massive steel hull of the *Princess Sophia* went up and over the top of the reef that she now travelled along. She continued her violent journey until the propellers came clear of the water. Freed of any resistance from the water, they spun wildly on their shafts, screaming into the night air.

Princess Sophia was aground on Vanderbilt reef.

Up in the wheelhouse, the sudden impact had thrown Captain Locke, First Officer Shaw, and the ship's quartermaster to the deck. The three men picked themselves up and glanced around at the array of papers, pens, booklets, and navigational instruments that had been thrown to the floor. Out on deck the two lookouts rushed to the side of the ship where, through the darkness, they could see the ocean crashing and receding from a stationary object beneath their keel: the rocky skeleton of Vanderbilt Reef.

Feeling the vibration from the wildly spinning screws, Captain Locke immediately rang "all stop" on the engine room telegraph. The comfortable *whump, whump, whump* of the ship's engines was replaced with the sounds of the wind howling through the rigging and ripping across the decks. But there was another, far more unsettling, noise that quickly filled their ears after the engines stopped: a low, creaking death rattle that came from deep within *Princess Sophia*'s hull and reverberated about every space on board. Made up of straining woodwork, scraping steel, and the dull, thunder-like noise of the sea coming in contact with her keel, the sound was the ship literally being twisted around on Vanderbilt Reef like a cork by the swirling seas and relentless winds.

Princess Sophia's 278 passengers had been fast asleep in their warm staterooms, but were quickly awoken by the collision. Sudden and violent, the impact threw many people from their berths to the floor of their small staterooms. In the darkness they fumbled for the switches that would activate the electric lights. They also sought out the solace of others; doors were quickly opened and heads poked out into corridors. John (Jack) Maskell, a thirty-one-year-old from England who was travelling to Manchester, looked out from his own stateroom to see that many women had emerged into the corridor clad only in their nightgowns. Some were crying while others stood in the windowless corridor, frozen in an apparent state of semi-shock.

In the age before public address systems, news of the accident travelled solely by word of mouth. Throughout the *Princess Sophia*'s passenger corridors, people were conferring as to what, if anything, they should do next. Lifebelts were generally felt to be a prudent idea, and the ship became a hive of activity, with stateroom doors clattering open and shut. United States Army Private Auris McQueen witnessed two women faint in front of him, while another began to change from her night clothes into her best formal black dress in the middle of the corridor, unconcerned as to who, if anyone, might be watching.

Still, despite the tense faces and worried looks worn by his fellow guests, McQueen noted that there was no panic among the passengers of the *Princess Sophia*. Clad in warmer clothing and strapped into their lifebelts, many began to make their way above decks for the evacuation that, surely, was to follow such an unusual occurrence. The ship had developed a slight but perceptible list to port, and heavy seas continued to pound into her stern and sides, shaking her right down to the keel and amplifying the terrible sounds made by her hull as it struggled to cope with this newfound stress.

Around this time Captain Locke immediately ordered the lifeboats swung out and prepared for launching. *Princess Sophia*'s uppermost boat deck didn't travel the entire length of the ship; six lifeboats were mounted on the open deck area around the ship's wheelhouse, while an additional four were situated at her stern above the smoking room, which was separated spatially from the rest of the superstructure. This resulted in a cumbersome process of having to descend one deck, then re-ascend the ladders that led to the roof of the smoking room to swing the last two boats out. The spare boats would be placed in davits once the first two were successfully away.

On the roof of the chart room and the officer's quarters, just aft of the wheelhouse, were more lifesaving conveyances. Known informally as "approved buoyancies," these were largely kept on board as a last resort. Comprised of two copper cylinders filled with air, they could support twenty-six people if needed, and could be launched by simply throwing them down from the ship's uppermost deck into the water. The drawback, particularly in the frigid waters of Alaska, is that these buoyancies were never intended to keep people dry, they were designed to act as a sort of mass flotation device, with ropes fitted to the two copper cylinders that could be held onto by swimmers in the water. Even if there had not been a storm battering the *Princess Sophia*, taking to the water in one of these during the fading days of October in Lynn Canal would have been tantamount to suicide.

High atop *Princess Sophia*'s exposed boat deck, wrestling with the lifeboats was cold, difficult exercise for the ship's crew. Near-blizzard conditions continued to obscure visibility, and high winds and heavy seas slammed into the ship with frightening regularity. Still, the crew — many of whom were little more than young men — worked diligently to prepare the boats and swing them out. During this time a few passengers likely wandered up on deck, but most probably retreated into the ship's public rooms, where they would have been sheltered from the elements. A few hearty individuals may have gone one deck down, where a semi-enclosed promenade provided some protection from the driving snow.

While this was taking place, Captain Locke summoned wireless operator David Robinson to send the call for help. Under Locke's direction, Robinson first sent a wireless message to the United States radio station in Juneau via the ship *Cedar*, which was anchored near Juneau harbour. Identifying *Princess Sophia* by her call letters, VFI, the

message stated they'd run aground on Vanderbilt Reef and asked any and all ships nearby to stop what they were doing and come to their aid. The time was fifteen minutes past two in the morning.

Even in 1918 the wireless was still in its infancy, and sending a message directly to the line's headquarters in Victoria — over 800 miles to the south — was simply not an option. Instead, Robinson had to rely on the *Cedar* and the wireless station in Juneau to send messages north to Skagway, where Lewis Johnston would soon be roused from his sleep, and south to the Canadian Pacific offices in Victoria.

In the darkened city of Juneau lights started popping on in homes just after three in the morning as the incredible news began to filter in, much of it in quick, informal wireless conversations that would only be recorded in shorthand in the Juneau Radio log book. These initial messages were short and to the point. They also revealed something of the workload on board *Princess Sophia* at a time when it was unclear to what extent she'd been damaged in the collision. Robinson was keeping his words brief. One of the first messages to go out simply stated, "*Princess Sophia* on Vanderbilt Reef calling for help." [1]

Over the next hour, Robinson would tap out six separate variations of this message. At 2:55 a.m. the situation on board appeared to be worsening, with Robinson wiring the Juneau office that the ship was "pounding heavily and lowering boats." [2]

At least, getting the passengers into the lifeboats was the plan. Slowly, one at a time, *Princess Sophia*'s white lifeboats — weighing roughly 1,700 tons apiece — were swung out

A Marconi operator at his post aboard the North German Lloyd liner *Grosserkorfurst*. Early shipboard wireless telegraphy was far from an exact science, and prone to dropouts and delays.

on their davits so that they extended over the side of the ship. Although their canvas covers remained on to protect them from the elements, they were ready to be embarked and lowered at a moment's notice. But in the face of the storm that raged on unabated, they were beginning to look about as enticing as the buoyancy rafts secured to the roof of the officers' quarters. Enveloped in total darkness and with the jagged rocks of Vanderbilt Reef immediately below the hull of the still-twisting ship, it was quickly becoming apparent that abandoning the *Princess Sophia* was not really an option at all.

On land, Frank Lowle, Canadian Pacific's agent in Juneau, was one of the first people to learn of the tragedy when his phone rang at 2:15 a.m. At first he almost didn't quite believe what he was hearing; a quick look outside his window revealed the weather in Juneau to be overcast but fair. The conditions that the *Princess Sophia* had been battling all night had yet to reach the city.

Hanging up, he rubbed the sleep from his eyes and mentally steeled himself for the start of a very long day. With over three hundred souls stranded on board the stricken vessel, Lowle knew that any rescue attempts would have to be mounted by a flotilla of smaller vessels. At this time of year the largest steamers that could have rendered assistance had the accident happened during the summer months had all gone south for the winter. There was one ship, however, that Lowle realized could help: the eighty-five-foot *Peterson*. She had just left Juneau the previous evening bound for Haines, Alaska, a small village on the western side of Lynn Canal just south of Skagway. Lowle picked the receiver back up and rang the up the cable

office. He requested the operator immediately telegraph the cable office in Haines. Despite the early hour, Lowle had heard a rumour that the Marconi operator there frequently slept in the office, not far from his set.

This innocuous action created yet another bizarre twist in what was already becoming an eventful Thursday morning. As it turned out the Marconi operator in Haines did not spend the night at the cable office, which was completely empty when the message from Juneau started to come in. For some inexplicable reason, at 2:45 a.m. in the morning on a cold October day, a passerby happened to be walking near the Marconi office when the telegraph from Juneau came through. The message coming through was bleak: "*Princess Sophia* ashore on Vanderbilt Reef, calling help; hasten Peterson to oblige Canadian Pacific Railway."[3] Only twenty-five minutes after Lowle passed the message along from Juneau, the word was out. *Princess Sophia* was in danger of sinking.

As if on cue, the *Peterson* came alongside in Haines. Her captain, Cornelius Stidham, immediately recruited two more crew members to help his existing complement of eight men, and had fifty extra blankets placed on board. History doesn't record how exactly the good captain procured these items during these small hours of the day, but by 4:00 a.m. *Peterson* was manoeuvring away from the dock in Haines and back out into the turbulent waters of Lynn Canal. The operator in Haines wired back the news to Frank Lowle in Juneau: the *Peterson* was coming.

Around the same time the *Peterson* set sail from Haines, help was also on the way from Juneau in the form of a small, sixty-five-foot mail boat called the *Estebeth*. Manned by Captain James Davis, the *Estebeth* was just four months old when she began her journey out of Juneau Harbor. She normally stuck to short mail and passenger runs between Juneau, Skagway, and the village of Sitka, located on the eastern side of Baranof Island near the Pacific Ocean. But if Captain Davis had qualms about pushing his new ship to her limits in a rescue attempt in bad weather, he kept his misgivings to himself. Although only licensed for thirty-five passengers, she could fit two hundred souls on board in a pinch. She would be the first of many vessels to leave Juneau Harbor in the hours before dawn that day.

Much like Frank Lowle when he looked out his window earlier that morning, Captain Davis only saw softly falling snow on his departure from Juneau. The weather the *Princess Sophia* was being punished with seemed to not be an issue at all. That all changed once the *Estebeth* cleared the northernmost point of Douglas Island. Here, at the entrance to Lynn Canal, Davis got a taste of what the stricken ship was facing. Snowfall increased dramatically and a strong wind from the north slammed into the ship's forward superstructure. Whipped up into a froth by the increasing wind, the heavy seas tossed the petite *Estebeth*. It took nearly six more hours of sailing through these conditions for her to reach the *Princess Sophia*.

Other vessels were on the way, and would arrive earlier. At 5:45 a.m. Juneau Radio wired David Robinson on board the *Princess Sophia*. "Tell VFI [*Princess Sophia*] [that] agent says three boats should arrive there in thirty minutes. These can care for 200 passengers." Robinson wired back almost immediately: "VFI [*Princess Sophia*] says there is danger of fuel tanks puncturing. Tide is rising and heavy sea running and strong wind on quarter. Stopped snowing."[4]

Four hours after running aground, this was the new challenge facing the *Princess Sophia*: whether or not the imminent high tide would force her off Vanderbilt Reef. Although the snow had let up and the fog that had enveloped them was finally beginning to lift, the wind and seas surrounding them remained as fearsome as ever. This concern filtered down to her passengers, most of whom were still huddled in the ships public rooms, strapped into their lifebelts. Fearing the worst, they began to make their way out on deck. For Captain Locke and his officers, how much damage the grounding had done to the ship's hull was still unknown. During their inspections of the ship's interior spaces it became clear she was not taking on water and her double-bottom hull had not been penetrated. This, however, was no safeguard against what might happen at high tide. As Army Private Auris McQueen noted, "It was thought she might pound her bottom out on the rocks."[5]

At six in the morning the tide hit its highest point. If anything, the increasing water level only managed to drive the wreck more firmly up on Vanderbilt Reef. The crashing of the waves against the hull and the horrifying sounds it created seemed to be lessening, and the weather was slowly starting to improve. Coupled with the assurances of Captain Locke and his officers and crew, most passengers began to calm down. Word had spread around the ship that other vessels were on their way, and most calculated that their situation seemed to be slowly improving. Many took off their lifebelts and conversed with each other, while card games broke out here and there using decks of Canadian Pacific-brand playing cards.

Satisfied that they were stuck on the reef for some time to come, at 7:20 a.m. the first formal wireless message of the entire day was sent out. Relayed from Captain Locke aboard the *Princes Sophia* via the United States Radio Station in Juneau, its recipient was Canadian Pacific's British Columbia coastal service superintendent, Captain James Troup.

PRINCESS SOPHIA RAN ON VANDERBILT REEF LYNN CANAL AT 3 O'CLOCK SHIP NOT TAKING WATER AND WATER UNABLE TO BACK OFF AT HIGH WATER FRESH NORTHERLY WIND SHIP POUNDED ASSISTANCE ON WAY FROM JUNEAU. LOCKE.[6]

In the wireless message the time is given as three in the morning. British Columbia was on Pacific Standard Time, which is one hour ahead of Alaskan Standard Time. *Princess Sophia* kept her clocks set to Pacific Standard Time, accounting for the difference. Unfortunately, wireless telegraphy was far from being an accurate science; the message sent to Captain Troup was received in Juneau at 7:20 a.m., but it wasn't passed along to the Canadian Pacific offices in Victoria until 8:24 a.m. Captain Troup finally received the message at 9:11 a.m. — nearly two full hours after it had been sent from the *Princess Sophia*. The delays and limitations of the wireless would continue to be a source of frustration and confusion as the day progressed.

Daylight — or what little ambient light could break through the suffocating greyness of the overcast skies — arrived just before eight in the morning. The snow had almost stopped, with just a few light flakes swirling about.

The wind still pounded at the stern of the ship. Finally Captain Locke could see well enough to properly assess the damage to his ship.

At 9:00 a.m. the *Peterson* arrived. At eighty-five feet, the *Peterson* was a steam-powered United States harbour boat, capable of making ten knots. But with no wireless apparatus on board, Stidham wasn't able to communicate with the outside world; any outgoing messages would have to be passed on via the *Princess Sophia* herself.

Princess Sophia looked different than the last time Stidham had laid eyes on her. Just the morning before, when *Princess Sophia* had docked in Juneau en route to Skagway, Captain Stidham had procured some much-needed oil from the ship. Looking at the massive Canadian Pacific ship perched high atop Vanderbilt Reef, the United States harbour boat captain tried to take it all in.

His thoughts turned to taking *Princess Sophia*'s passengers off. In a pinch, he could cram around one hundred twenty-five people on board the sturdy little *Peterson*, and Stidham reckoned he could potentially squeeze one hundred and fifty on board if he got creative. He might have to; a quick scan of the cloudy horizon revealed his ship was the first, and only, ship on the scene.

Ordering one of his crew, Kramer, to grab a megaphone, Stidham — who was at the helm of the *Peterson* and unable to leave his post — instructed him to hail the *Princess Sophia*. Almost immediately Captain Locke appeared on the open quarterdeck of his ship. Stidham instructed Kramer to ask Captain Locke if there was anything he could do. Through his own megaphone, Locke hollered back that he wanted the *Peterson* to remain close at hand. Leaning against the rail and gesturing down at the reef below his keel, Captain Locke responded that he was waiting for the tide to come in. At the moment, only *Princess Sophia*'s aftermost lifeboats could actually reach the water.

As he came closer, Stidham noticed that a large number of passengers had gathered at the rail on *Princess Sophia*'s promenade and boat decks. Dressed warmly, they peered out at the new arrival from their perch. One of her lifeboats, the third from the bow on the starboard side with three or four men in it, had been completely lowered to the water and was bobbing up and down alongside the *Princess Sophia*, still attached to its lines. Stidham realized they were crew members inspecting the hull of the ship, though they seemed to be spending much of their time just trying to keep the small boat from crashing into the steel hull. Stidham glanced up again at the passengers on the decks above him. None said a word.

Robert Wakely, *Peterson*'s engineer, also noticed the successfully lowered lifeboat. He was joined on deck by fellow crewmember Thomas Ryan, who noticed that *Princess Sophia* was leaking oil. The slick ran for well over a mile out from the wreck, and Ryan observed that the Canadian Pacific ship's bow had been torn away at the keel.

The two men looked at the lifeboat, resting calmly in the water with its small complement of crew members fussing about inside. Aside from the oil slick and the wind, conditions seemed good for a rescue attempt. The last seventy feet of the *Princess Sophia*'s hull rested comfortably in the water, off the reef. That should have been enough to get the aftermost lifeboats launched and to the rescue ships. But in a world still highly regulated by chain of command, neither Wakely nor Ryan said anything.

Fireman Victor Shockway also thought the time had come to get passengers off the *Princess Sophia*, but he was also reluctant to voice his opinion to Captain Stidham. "I didn't think it was any of my business," he would later say. "I don't go in where I ain't got no business."[7]

Recognizing that Captain Locke wanted the tide to rise so he could properly get *Princess Sophia*'s lifeboats in the water all at once, Captain Stidham manoeuvred the *Peterson* around the stricken ship, planning to stay close by until the next high tide. Stidham discussed the situation with the rest of his crew and they agreed that conditions were optimal for a rescue. Hopefully they would still be at high tide.

Despite there finally being the potential of rescue, many passengers were not so certain the danger was behind them. Even without the driving snow, the weather still bordered on atrocious, and the falling tide meant that more of Vanderbilt Reef — and the *Princess Sophia* — was being exposed.

One skeptic was Jack Maskell. The resident of Dawson City was travelling back to England to be with his fiancée, Dorothy. Grabbing a pen and some of the stationery paper that Canadian Pacific supplied, he found himself a comfortable spot in the observation room and sat down. From there he could gaze through the oversized windows showcasing a panoramic view of the bow and the ship's promenade deck. He twisted the pen around in his hand for a few moments. There was something about putting ink to paper that seemed to finalize things. Finally, he wrote:

To whom it may concern:
Should anything happen to me, notify Eagle Lodge, Dawson. My insurance, finances and property I leave to my wife (who was to be) Miss Dorothy Burgess, 37 Smart St., Longsight, Manchester, England.[8]

He signed the bottom of the page and noted the date in the top right-hand corner, adding "In Danger at Sea. Princess Sophia." He looked at the paper again and thought of Dorothy, thousands of miles away. Folding the note into neat sections, he tucked it into the pocket of his jacket. Silently, he took a fresh piece of paper and penned a second letter. This one was longer and far more personal.

Shipwrecked off Coast of Alaska. S.S. *Princess Sophia*. 24th Oct. 1918.
My own dear sweetheart,
I am writing this dear girl while the boat is in grave danger. We struck a rock last night which threw many from their berths, women rushed out in their night attire, some were crying, some too weak to move, but the life boats were soon swung out in all readiness, but owing to the storm would be madness to launch until there was hope for the ship, surrounding ships were notified by wireless and in three hours the first steamer came but cannot get near owing to the storm raging and the reef which we are on. There are now seven ships near. When the tide went down two thirds of the boat was high and dry. We are expecting the lights to go out any minute also the fires. The boat might go to pieces for the force of the waves are terrible, making awful noises on the side of the boat which has quite a list to port. No one is allowed to sleep, but believe me dear Dorrie it might have been much worse. Just here there is another big steamer coming. We struck the reef in a terrible snow storm. There is a life buoy marking the danger but the Captain was to port instead to starboard of buoy. I made my will this morning leaving everything to you my own true love and I want you to give £100 to my dear mother, £100 to my dear father, £100 to dear wee Jack and the balance of my estate (about £300) goes to you Dorrie dear. The Eagle Lodge will take care of my remains.[9]

He looked the letter over, then, satisfied, folded and placed it in his jacket pocket. Maskell didn't know it at the time, but the letters he had just completed would provide some of the only insight into what was actually taking place on board the *Princess Sophia* during her final hours.

Around the time Jack Maskell was penning his letter, the sixty-five-foot *Estebeth* arrived, coming up on the starboard side of *Princess Sophia*. After sailing for six straight hours from Juneau to aid the stricken ship, *Estebeth*'s captain, James Davis, made a new entry in his log book: "10:20 Wreck S.S. *Sophia*, Vanderbilt Reef." He then turned his attention to the *Princess Sophia*. He was surprised to see just how high out of the water she was resting; nearly the entirety of her bow was clear and surrounded by reef, while she sagged at the stern. All the way aft her propeller was visible above the waterline, though the majority of the bladed apparatus remained submerged. Of greater concern

Princess Sophia aground on Vanderbilt Reef. The strength of the wind can be seen by looking at her funnel – steam from the ship's generators is being blown nearly horizontal.

to Davis was the gash in her hull plating. It was expelling an enormous amount of water, somewhere in the neighbourhood of "two to three hundred gallons a minute — something like that — in a four to six inch stream."[10]

Captain Davis also noticed one of *Princess Sophia*'s lifeboats — the third from the bow on her starboard side — had been lowered approximately halfway down the side of the ship. Davis could see the shadowy black outline of people in it, and noticed others had gathered up near the bow on the ship's sunken well deck.

With the wind blowing fifteen to twenty miles, Captain Davis believed a rescue might be in progress. As he manoeuvred the *Estebeth* closer to the wreck, his brother and a local Juneau doctor who had been travelling with him stepped out on deck. The snow had stopped and the seas were calmer, with little more than wavelets disturbing the surface. The Davis brothers had the foresight to bring a very important piece of equipment with them on this rescue mission: a camera. Steadying it against the portside rail of the *Estebeth*, Davis's brother snapped the first shot of the stricken *Princess Sophia* up on Vanderbilt Reef: smoke wafting lazily from her funnel and a handful of whitecaps crashing on the reef.

Lying halfway between the *Estebeth* and the *Princess Sophia* was the triangular safety buoy, supposedly placed there to keep ships from running aground in the first place. A few more photographs were snapped and then *Estebeth*'s engines were powered up.

As Davis guided the *Estebeth* within two hundred feet of *Princess Sophia*, he hollered out to the ship. Captain Locke stepped out onto the starboard side of the open deck near the wheelhouse. Cupping his hands to his mouth, Davis shouted as loudly as he could so as to be heard over the wind: "Is an evacuation in progress?"

Locke replied that there wasn't. The crew had lowered the lifeboat to inspect the hull of the ship. This was the same one the crew of the *Peterson* had noticed an hour earlier. Locke shouted through his megaphone that they were resting securely on the reef for now, but asked the *Estebeth* to stay close. His plan, should the weather allow for it, was to hold tight until the wind let up a little more. Locke told Davis that once that happened he wanted the *Estebeth* to come around to the port side to assist in the evacuation.

Captain Locke looked down on the *Estebeth*, then shouted through his megaphone: "Do you think the wind will go down?" Davis yelled "No!" at the top of his lungs.

The *Estebeth* didn't have a megaphone or a wireless set and his words, drowned out by the still-howling wind and surf, failed to reach Captain Locke. After a few seconds of silence, Locke repeated the question through his megaphone. This time, on the *Estebeth*, Captain Davis vigorously shook his head back and forth; the international signal for "No."[11]

Not only was Davis doubtful the winds would go down, but he actually felt there was a good chance they would increase. Based on his past experiences with Lynn Canal, Davis knew that a strong north wind at this time of year, coupled with the heavy snow they'd already seen, seldom relented for long. Unable to properly communicate with Captain Locke, and with Locke reluctant to order an evacuation despite the improvement in the weather, Davis could do nothing for the moment. He guided the *Estebeth* farther away from the wreck, to the government buoy bobbing around in the swell, where he tied his ship up to await further instructions.

But by the time the *Estebeth* had been secured, Davis was beginning to worry again. The weather could change at any moment. If that happened any rescue attempt would be impossible. At 11:00 a.m., only forty minutes after arriving on the scene, Davis swung *Estebeth*'s skiff out and had it lowered to the water. He rationalized that if he could make it to the stricken *Princess Sophia*, he could use his skiff to begin taking passengers off. The wind, though, continued to gust well past twenty miles an hour. Despite vigorous rowing, Davis's hands were quickly becoming frozen and he was making little to no headway in approaching the wreck. Disheartened, he returned to the *Estebeth*, but left the skiff up on the ship's forward hatch in case they needed to launch it rapidly at some point.

Back in Juneau, Frank Lowle had been working non-stop to transfer messages to and from Canadian Pacific headquarters in Victoria, and to make arrangements in local hotels for *Princess Sophia*'s passengers, who would all need a place to stay when they were brought ashore. His mind, though, was never far from the stricken ship. Lowle messaged Captain Locke. He first asked the captain if there was anything in particular he needed at the moment. The reply came back negative. Lowle then wired Captain Locke the latest update on the rescue vessels he could expect to see:

BOATS PETERSEN, AMY, ESTEBETH, AND LONE FISHERMAN SENT IN ORDER GIVEN. WERE ONLY ONES AVAILABLE IMMEDIATELY. KING & WINGE LEAVES HERE AT ELEVEN THIS MORING, NOTHING ELSE POSSIBLE OF ANY SIZE. JEFFERSON RETURNED SEATTLE FROM SWANSON BAY. ADVISE ME RELATIVE DISPOSITION OF PASSENGERS FOR SUITABLE ARRANGEMENTS HERE.[12]

Getting the *King & Winge* to participate in the rescue effort had been harder than Lowle had anticipated. Earlier that morning Lowle had asked his assistant, Mr. Smeaton, to telephone her captain, thirty-six-year-old James Miller, just as the ship had arrived in Juneau with a hold full of freshly caught fish. A master mariner for seven years who had been at sea since the age of fourteen, Captain Miller told Lowle's assistant "to call up our agent and ask them if they [the crew] had to go on taking the fish out."[13] Miller knew his catch had to be unloaded and dried. Its potential loss would cost the company dearly, and he wasn't about to shirk his responsibilities. He may

have been captain of the *King & Winge*, but he was most definitely not her owner.

He was also not Frank Lowle's employee, and the Canadian Pacific agent found he had little sway over the loyal Captain Miller. Although Miller's own agent was located right in Juneau, Lowle and his assistant were unable to track him down as the morning went on. Lowle continued to badger the captain of the *King & Winge* to drop everything and set sail immediately, but Miller continued to defer to his local agent.

At 10:00 a.m., with his catch unloaded, Miller walked up the street to see Frank Lowle at his office. The young captain asked Lowle if he still wanted the *King & Winge* to set sail and steam toward the *Princess Sophia*. "Yes, I certainly do," he told Captain Miller pointedly. "And every boat I can get. Captain Locke says to send all the boats we can, and he thinks he can get off the reef at high water."[14]

As she finally got underway from Juneau, *King & Winge* also carried a civilian passenger on board who in the days to come would prove a valuable addition. Hearing about the unfolding disaster, Juneau-based photographer Pond walked down to the wharf and arranged to travel to the wreck aboard the *King & Winge* in order to take photographs of the rescue operations. Joining him was J. Clark Readman, a Juneau-based accountant who amused himself in his off hours as an amateur reporter for one of the local papers. Now, with Juneau receding into the distance behind them, both men prepared for the long afternoon of sailing ahead of them. They wouldn't reach *Princess Sophia* until well into evening.

The *King & Winge* would play a crucial role in the attempted rescue of those aboard the stricken *Princess Sophia*.

Back on Vanderbilt Reef, Captain Locke was in a quandary. The weather seems to have let up enough for a rescue mission to be possible. But he stood on the boat deck, surveying the motley assortment of marine craft scattered around his ship with growing anxiety. None of the vessels on-hand were large enough to take everyone off

the *Princess Sophia* in one go, and passengers would have to be taken to the rescue ships in several small lifeboats. If the weather took a turn for the worse while the small chain of lifeboats was making their way to or from the rescue vessels the results could be disastrous. Locke knew that you don't have to spend a lot of time in the water to succumb to hypothermia. If only he had more ships standing by....

Striding across the deck, Captain Locke put his head into the wireless room and asked wireless operator David Robinson to message Jack Lowle in Juneau. Robinson immediately did so, advising Lowle that the four vessels currently on scene would not be adequate enough to transport all passengers and crew.

U.S.S. PETERSON & OTHER SEVERAL SMALL GAS BOATS STANDING BY. WANT ALL BOATS AVAILABLE TAKE OFF PASSENGERS.[15]

An hour later, Captain Locke received a positive reply from Lowle in Juneau:

CANNERY TENDERS EXCURSION AND ELSINORE LEFT AT 11:45 THIS MORNING FOR YOU. ADVISE ME YOUR PLANS FOR CARE PASSENGERS OR PROSPECTS YOUR BOATS TAKING THEM.[16]

Cannery tenders were small vessels intended to support larger fishing vessels. In 1918 plenty of older fishing ships still used sail power, and it wasn't uncommon for a cannery tender to tow fishing vessels operating under sail to the grounds, in order to save time. Designed to shuttle the catch from the grounds to the canneries on shore, they were small and nimble. Both the *Excursion* and *Elsinore* probably only carried a crew of four men each, at best, but their small size meant they could potentially get closer to the *Princess Sophia* than other vessels. If the weather held, Captain Locke likely reckoned he could at least get a few passengers off his stricken ship.

At noon an entirely different problem presented itself to the passengers and crew on board *Princess Sophia*

— though those without a maritime background likely didn't take notice. Low tide had officially reached the *Princess Sophia*, but with that came the realization that her hull was no longer being supported at the stern by the buoyancy of the water. Private Auris McQueen described it as a tense, unpredictable time:

The most critical time, nobody but the ship's officers, we soldiers and a few sailors amongst the crew and passengers were told of it, was at low tide at noon when the captain and chief officer figured she was caught on the starboard bow and would hang there while she settled on the port side and astern. They were afraid she would turn turtle, but the bow pounded around and slipped until she settled into a groove, well supported forward on both sides.[17]

The danger quickly passed, but McQueen noticed that aside from the frightful noises coming from her hull as the waves pushed her around on the reef, the *Princess Sophia* seemed very sturdy. Surely it was safer on board this gigantic liner, sheltered from the elements, than out in the swirling ocean on an exposed lifeboat. McQueen's fellow passengers, undisturbed by the noise except for the odd shudder that interrupted those writing letters and shook the frame of the vessel, began to slip into this modified shipboard routine. With the arrival of each new vessel, passengers would gather on deck to watch it approach with a feeling of both relief and anxiety.

Shortly before 2:00 p.m., on the *Estebeth*, Captain Davis perked up when he saw *Princess Sophia*'s starboard aft shell doors suddenly swing open. The number of people on the deck had dramatically increased, and a ladder had been swung into position. The half-lowered lifeboat that had been at the ship's side earlier in the morning now rested underneath the ladder, and Davis quickly started his engines as he saw roughly fifteen passengers begin to make their way down the ladder.

As the *Estebeth* untied and motored away from the buoy, the partially lowered lifeboat started to move. Ever so gingerly it inched its way toward the water. Captain Davis picked up speed; he wanted to meet the boat as soon as possible.

When the *Estebeth* was sixty feet from the wreck and closing, something happened that surprised Captain Davis: the lifeboat, which had been resting fully in the water with a small complement of passengers, suddenly began to ascend back up to the boat deck. When the lifeboat was about six feet above the waterline the crew on deck stopped hoisting, and the lifeboat rested there in her davits for a few seconds. Finally, after what seemed like an interminable wait, the crew on deck began to hoist again. One by one, each passenger got out of the lifeboat and disappeared back through the shell doors and inside the *Princess Sophia*. While they waited, they looked down over the side of the lifeboat at Captain Davis and the *Estebeth*. No one spoke.

At this point, Captain Locke came out on the open deck outside the bridge. Shouting through his megaphone, a weary Locke warned Captain Davis to keep the *Estebeth* away from the rocks. As Davis would later recount, Captain Locke felt the *Estebeth* was coming too close, and that she was "in danger."[18]

Discouraged and annoyed, Captain Davis would spend the next four hours slowly guiding the *Estebeth* to the stern of the *Princess Sophia* before allowing the current to push her back through the water near the starboard side of the ship. He'd repeat this tedious process all afternoon, wanting to "stay close to her to see if they wouldn't get up courage enough to transfer the passengers, or do something."[19]

Davis knew there was a safe landing site just eight or ten miles away from the *Princess Sophia*'s current location, where passengers could be safely offloaded before being transported on larger vessels to Juneau. A cannery in nearby Tee Harbor would have provided shelter and a much-needed staging area. Unfortunately, he was powerless over Captain Locke. Regardless of the situation on the much-larger *Princess Sophia*, Captain Locke was in command there — not Captain Davis. However small, the seeds of doubt had been sown in James Davis's mind. In a few short months he'd be pressed to give his assessment of the surreal moment when the potential salvation of those still-stranded passengers slipped through his fingers. When asked what other master mariners would have thought of Captain Leonard Locke's decision to sit tight, Davis was blunt. "Some people would call others in for consultation," he said. "Others would not. Personally, I think if a master has no confidence in his own judgement, he is unfit to be the master of a ship."[20]

Another person beginning to doubt Captain Locke's assessment of the situation was Captain Cornelius Stidham. From the wheelhouse of the *Peterson*, he saw that the number of passengers on deck had suddenly increased. Not only were more people crowding *Princess Sophia*'s open decks than two hours ago, but Stidham observed that many of them were now clutching suitcases and other personal belongings. With high tide having just arrived, evacuation again looked imminent. The time was 4:30 p.m.

Captain Stidham waited for a sign. And waited. Despite the influx of excitement on the open decks, no signal came from the *Princess Sophia*. The *Peterson* lacked a wireless, and could not message the *Princess Sophia* directly. Moreover, Stidham — like most mariners — believed it was beyond his scope to publicly question Captain Locke's decision-making or authority. As far as he was concerned, the *Peterson* was there to help — but only when help is formally requested. "We went there to perform services," he would later say. "If the master of the vessel didn't take advantage of it, it would not be our fault … Captain Locke had better lifeboats than I had at the time; he had larger ones, and it was his place to have the lifeboats put over — it wasn't my place to have put them over."[20]

In any event, the evacuation appeared to be a false alarm. By five that evening, most of those stranded on board the *Princess Sophia* began to disperse from the open decks, heading below into the warm, brightly lit public rooms. A few stragglers remained on deck for a while, clinging to luggage and hope, before they too relented. By the time the sun set, one fact was glaringly obvious to Captain Stidham: any hope of rescue would not come tonight.

Just after 6:00 p.m., the *Peterson* manoeuvred up to the *Princess Sophia*. The weather, which had been calm up until about 4:30 p.m., had begun to worsen, and Captain Stidham wanted to know whether his assistance was still needed. Just as he had done seven hours ago, he had deckhand Kramer hail Captain Locke on the ship's megaphone. Captain Locke appears on deck, silhouetted by the amber glow of the ship's exterior lighting. Through his own megaphone, Locke shouted down to Kramer and Captain Stidham. He was expecting a steamer to arrive later that night; the *Peterson* was free to seek shelter for the evening if she'd just stay by the *Princess Sophia* until the steamer arrived.

Twenty minutes later, the *King & Winge* reached Vanderbilt Reef, with the indefatigable Captain James Miller in command. He, too, had no wireless apparatus, and the growing darkness was making it impossible to get a decent look at the ship. Unable to get close enough to the *Princess Sophia* to hail Captain Locke, Miller sailed the *King & Winge* back and forth near the wreck in the hopes that the lights of his ship would provide some comfort to those still stranded on board.[21] The ship that Captain Locke had so eagerly requested that morning had arrived, and was completely unable to do anything to help. Locke now knew that he, along with every other passenger and crew member on board, must survive another night up on the reef.

At 8:00 p.m., on board the *Peterson*, Captain Stidham finally saw the lights of another ship approaching. It was the *Cedar*; a two hundred-foot United States Lighthouse steamer equipped with a wireless set.[22] With the winds intensifying, and satisfied that his help would not be needed during the night, Captain Stidham sailed the *Peterson* fourteen miles to Shelter Island, where he spent the night at anchor, protected from the worst of the weather.

Commanded by John Leadbetter, the *Cedar* was substantially larger than the other rescue ships that had been coming to and from the wreck throughout the day. As the largest tender ever built for the United States Lighthouse Service, her size and four on-board lifeboats could greatly expedite rescue efforts. In an emergency, up to four hundred people — everyone currently on board the *Princess Sophia* — could be placed aboard this one ship.

Approaching the wreck as close as he dared, Leadbetter shone his searchlights on the Canadian Pacific ship, illuminating her stranded hulk from the darkness that surrounded it. A strong wind from the northwest had picked back up and was whipping the water into little whitecaps that hit Leadbetter's searchlights, disintegrating into mist as the wind picked the spray up and flung it across the curved windows of the wheelhouse. The snow had also restarted and sporadic flakes joined the spray, obscuring his visibility. Leadbetter switched the searchlights off, and *Princess Sophia* disappeared momentarily. As his eyes adjusted to the darkness, only her running lights and deck lights could be seen.

Since the *Cedar* was equipped with a wireless apparatus, Leadbetter wired Captain Locke on the *Princess Sophia* to ask if her passengers were safe. Locke replied that they were. Leadbetter then had his wireless operator, Elwood Miller, ask Captain Locke if would he like the *Cedar* to standby and remain underway for the duration of the night, ready to assist; or could he anchor the *Cedar* on Benjamin Island, just a few nautical miles away?

Weary after a long day at the key tapping out emergency messages, the response from wireless operator Robinson was already unenthusiastic:

CAN ANCHOR IF CARE TO. CAN DO NOTHING TONIGHT.

The message had barely reached Miller's key when the lights on the ship they had been shadowing for a little over half an hour suddenly began to flicker. Without warning, they were completely extinguished. Not even the *Princess Sophia*'s running lights remained on. Noticing the change, Captain Leadbetter rushed to the windows and peered out into the darkness as Miller frantically began tapping out another message to Robinson. It went answered.

At 8:30 p.m. on Thursday, October 24, 1918, the 343 passengers and crew aboard the *Princess Sophia* were plunged into total darkness. It would be their longest — and last — night alive.

CHAPTER SEVEN
THE TURN
– STAR PRINCESS

0100 HRS, JUNE 23, 1995
ON BOARD *STAR PRINCESS* IN LYNN CANAL

On the starboard side of the darkened bridge on board Princess Cruises' *Star Princess*, Alaska State Pilot Robert Nerup quietly looked up from the radar console where he has been perched since his colleague, Pilot Ronald Kutz, had departed the bridge five minutes earlier. He was disturbed by what he saw on the radar, but a quick scan of the view wasn't all that helpful in the fading light. Something was amiss; the ship wasn't where he expected her to be. The mid-channel manoeuvre in Lynn Canal had left *Star Princess* about one nautical mile off her plotted course. To remedy the situation and bring *Star Princess* back on her intended track, Pilot Nerup ordered the vessel's course altered from 143°T to 126°T. The quartermaster complied, and *Star Princess* once again began to turn.

Fifteen minutes later, at 1:15 in the morning, Nerup put the electronic bearing line (EBL) on his radar. Intended to show the vessel's eventual track if maintained on any given course, the EBL is a useful tool for lining the ship up against a given radar plot. In this case, Nerup kept the EBL on the radar screen and ordered another course change, this time to 156°T — a heading he kept the *Star Princess* on until the EBL on his screen had passed over the location of the Poundstone Rock buoy.

Nerup believed that the thirty degree course correction should have placed *Star Princess* one full cable — six hundred feet — to the east of Poundstone Rock. Still not quite as much clearance as Pilot Nerup would have liked, so he ordered another course correction, this time to 155°T. He wanted *Star Princess* to pass at least two cables — twelve hundred feet — east of Poundstone Rock, the minimum safe distance Nerup was comfortable with. At this point passing to the west of Poundstone Rock was no longer an option. *Star Princess* was already crossing Vanderbilt Reef on the east side. "Once you pass Vanderbilt [on the east side]," he would later testify, "I don't feel that the option to go to west [of Poundstone Rock] is open any longer."[1]

Having sailed this route so many times in the past, Nerup likely knew about the *Princess Sophia* accident and the checkered history of Lynn Canal, but his colleagues on the bridge probably didn't realize their vessel was crossing over the graveyard of Alaska's worst maritime disaster. The bridge was silent as Vanderbilt Reef glided slowly past the ship's starboard side at 01:15 in the morning.

Ten minutes later another obstacle cropped up. Ahead of the *Star Princess* the deck and navigation lights of another vessel suddenly came into view. Pilot Nerup saw it and established that it was heading toward them based on the positioning of the ship's red and green navigation lights mounted to both the starboard and port-side bridge wings. It was still off in the distance — probably nine and a half miles — and looked to Nerup as if it was abeam of Aaron Island, six miles to the south of Sentinel Island.

The ship approaching them was the *Fair Princess* — a smaller, older cruise ship belonging to Princess Cruises. She was headed north through Lynn Canal bound for her scheduled port of call in Skagway, where she was due to arrive later on in the morning. As he watched the new ship, Nerup saw her navigation lights "open" — a term for when both the port and starboard navigation lights are no longer visible. Instead, Nerup saw the masthead light of the *Fair Princess*, along with her red port-side navigation light. The experienced Alaska State pilot assumed that *Fair Princess* had altered her course to allow for both vessels to pass port-to-port, or left side to left side.

Still, Pilot Nerup wasn't sure what exactly the *Fair Princess* intended to do. He couldn't tell if she intended to pass Poundstone Rock — which lay ahead of the *Star Princess* — on the east or west side. The previously plotted track for *Star Princess* called for the vessel to pass to the east of Poundstone Rock. As things stood, Nerup thought *Fair Princess* might attempt to squeeze through the channel on the eastern side of Poundstone Rock as well. Despite the uncertainty surrounding her intended course and actions, Pilot Nerup made no effort to call the *Fair Princess* using the ship's bridge-to-bridge VHF radiotelephone. Nerup assumed that both vessels were taking the appropriate actions to pass each other safely, and that no further clarification was needed. Essentially, he believed an accident was impossible.

Nerup's decision actually contravened the recommendations of the Bridge-to-Bridge Radiotelephone Act of the United States. Applicable to all vessels operating in navigable waters of the United States, the regulation requires vessels to transmit any and all information necessary for save navigation. Someone on either ship should have picked up the bridge-to-bridge radiotelephone. No one did. A single radio call would have told Pilot Nerup exactly what he needed to know. Instead, he continued to stare out the windows of the bridge, concentrating on what — if anything — the *Fair Princess* intended to do.

At 01:30, Third Officer Alcaras took another reading of the current position of the *Star Princess* and plotted it on the ship's navigation chart. He noticed that the ship is still roughly 0.3 miles west of her intended track, which had been approved by the master at the start of the season.

Third Officer Alcaras wasn't particularly concerned; the deviation was a minor one, and he had sailed with Pilot Nerup before. He glanced over at Nerup, who was staring intently out the window. Satisfied that the Alaska State pilot had the situation under control, Third Officer Alcaras returned to his charts.

Second Officer Landi also knew that his ship is running due west of where she should be, but he was also not concerned. Later, both Second Officer Landi and Third Officer Alcaras would testify that neither spoke up because Pilot Nerup "... was piloting the vessel. He [was] a professional; he [knew] where we should be. He [had] been [there] before [and] he [was] making the necessary course changes."[2]

As if to confirm both Second Officer Landi and Third Officer Alcaras's thoughts, Pilot Nerup ordered yet another course change at 01:35. He had the quartermaster place the *Star Princess* on a heading of 153°T. The helmsman complied, and *Star Princess* began to turn. The event is recorded on the ship's voyage event recorder (EVR), which had been monitoring and noting the ship's technical performance all evening.

Despite the course correction, the heading still left *Star Princess* on a course that was closer to the Poundstone Rock buoy than Pilot Nerup would've liked. On a heading of 153°T, the vessel will pass the buoy on her starboard side with less than two cables, or twelve hundred feet, of clearance. If the *Fair Princess* wasn't there, Nerup would have put *Star Princess* as much as eight degrees farther to the west, on a course of 145°T. But with the oncoming ship in his way, Pilot Nerup didn't have that option.

On board the *Fair Princess*, the pilot was able to visually identify *Star Princess*. Travelling at 17.5 knots through the darkness, she was travelling on her own constant heading of 336°T. The pilot aboard *Fair Princess* felt that both ships would pass with about half a mile in between them, at a point just south of Poundstone Rock. He noticed that *Star Princess* was travelling on a course that would take her very close to the Poundstone Rock buoy, but he did not attempt to call the ship to inquire if that was intentional. Like Pilot Nerup, the pilot on board the *Fair Princess* assumed the passage would go smoothly. Still, he made a point of not ordering any sudden or major course corrections that might spook the bridge team aboard *Star Princess* and give them reason to worry. Slow and steady wins this race.

At 01:40, Pilot Nerup stood up from his chair on the starboard side of the navigation bridge and walked over to the centre of the room. He stared out the window that ran directly along the centreline of the ship, overlooking the exact tip of the bow many decks below him. *Fair Princess* was two miles away and closing, and Nerup's attention was divided between the approaching ship and the oncoming buoy for Poundstone Rock.

Second Officer Landi was standing just to the right of Pilot Nerup, on the starboard side of the bridge near the navigation console. Third Officer Alcaras was hunched over the radar screen on the same side of the bridge. As it approached the ship, both Pilot Nerup and Second Officer Landi lost sight of the buoy. The time was 01:42.

Suddenly the routine silence on the bridge was shattered by a low, grinding, rumbling that came from deep within the hull. Second Officer Landi felt the floor shake. Pilot Robert Nerup felt it too and wondered what the problem was. He immediately made his way over to the starboard side of the bridge and opened the door to the exposed bridge wing. Second Officer Landi had also crossed over the wheelhouse floor, and joined Pilot Nerup on the starboard bridge wing. From their vantage point, high above the sea, both men were able to see the Poundstone Rock buoy glide underneath the bridge wing and begin to fall astern of the still-moving ship, which had dropped to a speed of just 3.5 knots in a matter of seconds.

Alaska State pilot Robert K. Nerup immediately realized what had happened. At almost two in the morning, while the majority of her passengers and crew were sleeping soundly, *Star Princess* had collided with Poundstone Rock. Nerup was sure of that. The real question was: how badly damaged was she?

CHAPTER EIGHT
STRANDED ON THE ROCKS — PRINCESS SOPHIA

When the lights went off aboard the *Princess Sophia*, everyone immediately assumed the worst. Aboard the *Cedar*, Captain Leadbetter's first thought was that the ship had begun to founder. Nearby, on the *King & Winge*, Captain Davis was thinking along similar lines. He had the engines put on "slow ahead" and gradually crept closer to the wreck, ordering his men to keep a watchful eye for any evacuation efforts.

Finally the lights aboard the *Princess Sophia* began to faintly flicker. "Every once in a while, we would see a faint light on the vessel, which would flicker and go out,"[1] said Juneau reporter and accountant J. Clark Readman. From his perch on the deck of the *King & Winge*, Readman tried to discern what, if anything, he was seeing amongst the blowing snow obscuring his vision. "We could not tell whether they were trying to put up rockets, or whether it was a lantern, or what it was. It was quite a faint light ... and things remained about in that condition until daylight."[2]

The sudden plunge into darkness had the same disconcerting effect on *Princess Sophia*'s passengers and crew. The darkness removed one of the few remnants of safety. Everyone was left fumbling around in the pitch-dark confines of the ship, causing many cries of confusion. Captain Locke quickly sent crew down into the hull to sound the ship. To his relief, they returned with the word that a steam pipe had broken, depriving *Princess Sophia* of fuel for her electrical generators. Locke and his officers quickly took charge, explaining the situation to the worried passengers crowding the ship's social hall and ornate staircase that ran between the awning and promenade decks. Lanterns were affixed to her exterior and interior decks until a permanent solution could be found.

Around 10:00 p.m., wireless operator Robinson got the *Princess Sophia*'s battery set to work long enough to tap out a message to Captain Leadbetter on the *Cedar*, the only vessel near the stricken ship that is also fitted with a wireless apparatus. The communication reaffirmed Leadbetter's

The *Cedar*, shown here in the mid-1930s, was commanded by the indefatigable Captain John W. Leadbetter at the time of the *Princess Sophia*'s sinking.

Few shots of the *Princess Sophia*'s interior spaces survive, but this shot of the forward lounge and staircase aboard *Princess May* are a near match in terms of the layout and interior design aboard the *Princess Sophia*.

belief that *Princess Sophia* was firmly wedged on Vanderbilt Reef. They agreed to attempt to take off passengers at four in the morning. At 11:45 p.m. the message was passed from Juneau Radio to Frank Lowle, Canadian Pacific's man in Juneau, who had been alternating between work and sleep all evening, along with his assistant, Smeaton. The two settled in to sleep in their offices until the rescue effort began in the early morning hours.

On Friday, October 25th, shortly after 4:00 a.m., Captain Leadbetter ordered the *Cedar*'s anchor raised. While snow squalls still obscured his view periodically, the real trouble was the wind, which had increased substantially since the night before and was whipping the seas into a frenzy. Captain Leadbetter guided the *Cedar* back toward Vanderbilt Reef, but was unable to see the *Princess Sophia*. Evidently the steam pipe had not yet been repaired, as her deck lights were still extinguished.

With her lights out and the weather worsening, the planned early morning rescue effort was abandoned before it could even start. At 5:50 a.m. the *Cedar* messaged Juneau Radio, stating that nothing could be done until daybreak at the very least, owing to the miserable sea conditions. The operator in Juneau passed the message on to Frank Lowle, advising him that the *Cedar* would provide another update at eight a.m. Lowle leaned back in his chair and rubbed his eyes; once again he was in the unenviable position of having to break the news to Captain James Troup, Canadian Pacific's superintendent of British Columbia coastal steamers.

In Victoria, Captain Troup's demeanour bordered on apoplectic. Wireless communications with Juneau had been unreliable at best, and what few messages were making it down to the provincial capital were almost universally bad news. While some messages made it through in decent time, others were getting garbled up or simply lost in the shuffle. On several occasions, Troup was simply unable to message Juneau due to the amount of wireless traffic zipping back and forth between the ships and the offices in Skagway, Juneau, and Victoria.

An excellent example of this had occurred the night before. At 7:00 p.m. Lowle sent a message to Captain Troup, advising him that *Princess Sophia* was resting securely on Vanderbilt Reef and was unable to float off at high tide. He outlined the various vessels that were around the stricken ship, standing by to take on passengers, but emphasized that this wasn't possible due to darkness and the increasingly poor weather conditions. By Friday morning that message still hadn't arrived in Captain Troup's hands. Although Lowle had left it with Juneau Radio, the Juneau office didn't find time to transmit it until 2:19 p.m., and it was four more hours before Captain Troup laid eyes on it. The total time for this wireless message, bearing Juneau serial number SRS 10825, to travel from point A to point B was a mind-numbing twenty-three hours.

————

At daybreak, Captain Leadbetter got his first good look at the *Princess Sophia*. Her entire bow was still completely clear of the water, and Leadbetter could see right down to her keel. He also noticed that even at almost high tide the water didn't even come within three feet of the draught marks that indicated the typical position of the waterline on the ship. Even more incredible, he noticed that the ship had managed to wedge herself into a crevasse on the reef, the sides of which rose up over eight feet above her keel.

Nearby, on the *King & Winge*, Captain James Miller noticed that the weather was vastly worse than the day before. Snow squalls developed and would blow hard for ten to fifteen minutes before disappearing again. Now that day had broken, Captain Miller manoeuvred his ship closer to the *Princess Sophia*. "I approached her as near as I could," said Miller. "I got within 200 yards of her — probably not that far — I could see the men on deck, and I could see that they had sailors suits on, so I must have been pretty close to her."[3]

Glancing up at the massive hulk resting on Vanderbilt Reef, it became obvious to Miller that nothing could be done to rescue her passengers; at least, not at the moment. Because of the reef, Miller couldn't bring the *King & Winge* close enough to the stricken *Princess Sophia* to be of much help. He thought it might be possible to run a line down from the ship to the *King & Winge* to help guide his lifeboats to retrieve passengers, but even they would not be able to get close enough to render assistance. Passengers would have to jump in the water and take the chance that they would be picked up before hypothermia set in.

Like Captain Leadbetter on board the *Cedar*, Captain James Miller decided he would wait near the wreck, hopeful for a break in the weather so that they could safely begin transferring passengers off the stranded Canadian Pacific liner. "We came to the conclusion that his [Locke's] passengers were safer on the ship than to try to transfer them on board our boats on account of the weather."[4]

The morning's abandoned evacuation efforts evidently changed little in the shipboard routine aboard the *Princess Sophia*. With nowhere to go and nothing to do, passengers once again attempted to busy themselves to pass the time as quickly as possible. Were it not for the reef underneath them and the harsh winter climate outside, they could have very well been sailing down the Inside Passage toward Vancouver: the usual socializing took place in the observation lounge on the promenade deck, while many of the men no doubt retreated farther aft, to the cigar and leather-clad smoking room located in a separate deck house at the stern.

Wherever thirty-five-year-old United States Army Private Auris McQueen decided to sit down and write shortly after eight in the morning, he was apparently quite comfortable. Gathering a pen and some paper, he wrote a candid letter to his mother, giving it the title "In the Lynn Canal Off Skagway" and noting the date: 10-25-18. Despite the fact that he had been stranded on board the *Princess Sophia* on Vanderbilt Reef for over thirty hours, his light mood was reflected in an opening joke:

The man who wrote "On a Slow Train Through Arkansas" could write a true story of a "Slow Trip Through Alaska" if he had been with a party of a few soldiers. We were sure making a slow trip. We were on a government steamer from Fort Gibbon to Whitehorse and had no pilot who knew the river, so had to tie up nights, and at that got stuck on six sand bars [sic].[5]

The smoking room aboard the *Princess May*, photographed in April 1903, would have been similar in design and appearance to the same space on board the *Princess Sophia*.

The journey continued to get more darkly comical for Private McQueen; the irony that he was on a steamer that had ground out hard on a reef in the middle of a storm was not lost on him. He and the small party of soldiers he was travelling with were so delayed on their riverboat trip down to Skagway that when they arrived there they missed three consecutive steamers south before Skagway's Canadian Pacific agent, Lewis H. Johnston, secured them passage aboard the *Princess Sophia*. In his letter, McQueen noted they only got on board the *Princess Sophia* "by good luck."[6]

Aside from the blackout, McQueen wrote to his mother that the only real inconveniences passengers had suffered up until then were the lack of fresh water on board and that the ship had run out of sugar. "But," he continued, "we still have lump sugar and water for drinking."[7] He also noted it had taken him a while to pen the letter, owing to the fact that the ship continued to be pounded and whipped about by the seas. He still closed jovially enough. "I'm going to go quit," he writes, "and see if I can rustle a bucket and a line to get some sea water to wash in."[8] If McQueen did manage to find the bucket and line he sought, he might have thought differently about washing in it: the temperature of the water outside was just above freezing. Still, before he rose from his chair and left the warmth of the lounge, he took the time to fold and tuck the note into his pocket.

In all likelihood, many passengers were either penning letters to loved ones during the morning hours or updating their personal journals with firsthand accounts of their adventures. Their personal stories, thoughts, and feelings will never be known. Jack Maskell and Auris McQueen had no way of knowing it at the time, but the letters they penned would form the only real insight into what was happening on board the stricken *Princess Sophia* — because they had the foresight to place their notes inside their clothing.

With the passengers doing their best to while away the long morning, shortly after 9:00 a.m. Frank Lowle messaged the *Princess Sophia* from Juneau. After having worked around the clock for over twenty-four hours with little to no sleep and under increasing pressure from Captain Troupe in Victoria, he was exasperated that his efforts had yet to yield any real results. Now he was at a loss for what to do:

I SENT OUT YESTERDAY THE GAS BOATS ESTEBETH, AMY, LONE FISHERMAN, ALSO KING AND WINGE AND CANNERY TENDERS EXCURSION AND ELSINORE. AMY CAME BACK THIS MORNING. ARE OTHERS THERE? TWO MEN ON LONE FISHERMAN HAVE NO GRUB. WOULD APPRECIATE ANY INSTRUCTIONS YOU MAY WISH TO GIVE ME. STANDARD OIL TANKER IS HERE. CAN YOU USE HER?[9]

Because of the continued problems with the steam pipe aboard *Princess Sophia*, it was four hours before the message reached her wireless operator, David Robinson. Having been awake since the accident occurred, Robinson was exhausted. Still, he kept trying to communicate with the *Cedar* using his battery backup.

Meanwhile the weather conditions outside were so awful that any rescue attempt was unthinkable. Winds gusting up to one hundred miles per hour tore through Lynn Canal and slammed into the *Cedar* and the *King & Winge*, which were still standing by to render assistance that was beginning to seem impossible. "I couldn't make my anchors hold," Captain Leadbetter would later say of the hefty *Cedar*.[10] He consulted quickly with Captain James Miller of the *King & Winge*, and both men agreed that it would only be a matter of time before they would have to seek shelter. Before doing so they did come up with a plan of action: fitted with a three-hundred-and-fifty-fathom anchor chain, the *King & Winge* would anchor near the stern of the *Princess Sophia* while the *Cedar* took up a position to the immediate west of her. From there they would run lines to the stern of the *Princess Sophia*, allowing the *Cedar*'s boats to run along this makeshift guideline and eliminating the need to launch *Princess Sophia*'s lifeboats. In conversation with Captain Locke, all three captains agreed that the current weather made rescue impossible. The next ideal time, they thought, would be around 4:30 p.m.

For the most part, *Princess Sophia* spent her last afternoon on Vanderbilt Reef alone, whipped by the monstrous gusts of wind that raced down Lynn Canal and pounded by the churning seas. Just after one in the afternoon the snow returned full force. Rather than abating, as Captain Locke had been hoping, the storm intensified with each passing minute. In Sitka the barometer had dropped dramatically by midday, making a major storm all but certain. Reflecting on the intensity of the storm later, Captain Leadbetter would call it "a strong blizzard as I ever saw in Lynn Canal. It was a date earlier than I ever saw before; 8th of November, I think, is the earliest."[11]

Nearby on the *King & Winge*, just before 11 a.m. Juneau photographer E.P. Pond mounted his camera on a tripod fixed to the ship's deck. Between the pitching ship he was standing on and the stationary one he was trying to photograph, Pond grasped the camera tightly in an attempt to gain a clear exposure. He rattled off a series of shots of the stricken *Princess Sophia* and hoped for the best. Little did he know that these photographs would show the ship's final hours. Compared to the photograph taken the previous morning by the Davis brothers on board the *Estebeth*, Pond's exposures would show a ship surrounded by a vengeful, angry sea, as if the *Princess Sophia* was about to be swallowed up into the gates of hell.

Around lunchtime the lights aboard the *Princess Sophia* blinked back on. The broken steam pipe had been repaired by the ship's understaffed three-man engineering team, who had worked tirelessly through the night to restore power. Now, smoke once again wafted from her funnel uptake, only to be pushed horizontally across the horizon as it emerges.

With the steam pipe patched up and electrical power restored to the *Princess Sophia*, Captain Locke had wireless operator David Robinson immediately message Captain Troup in Victoria, via Juneau Radio:

STEAMER CEDAR, THREE GAS BOATS STANDING BY. UNABLE TO TAKE OFF PASSENGERS ACCOUNT STRONG NORTHERLY GALE AND BIG SEA RUNNING. SHIP HARD AND FAST ON REEF WITH BOTTOM BADLY DAMAGED BUT NOT MAKING WATER, UNABLE TO BACK OFF REEF. MAIN STEAM PIPE BROKEN. DISPOSITION OF PASSENGERS NORMAL.[12]

Captain Locke also found the time to return Frank Lowle's earlier message, advising him that any and all rescue efforts were suspended until the weather moderated, and that the *Cedar* and *King & Winge* were standing by. Somewhat glibly, he also asked Lowle how the weather was in Juneau. Lowle didn't respond.

Captain Locke's assessment that the current disposition of his passengers was, as he put it, "normal," was surprisingly accurate. United States Army Private Auris McQueen's letter to his mother was focused more on the logistical challenges that lay between him and his final destination than on the predicament he found himself in.

As soon as this storm quits we will be taken off and make another lap to Juneau. I suppose after 3 or 4 days there, we can go to Seattle, after I reckon we will be quarantined, as there are six cases of influenza on board. The decks are dry, and this wreck has all the markings of a movie stage setting. All we lack is a hero and a vampire.[13]

McQueen even closed his letter with a darkly ominous line: "We are mighty lucky we were not all buried in the sea water."[14]

Nearby, on board the *Cedar*, Captain Leadbetter perked up as his ship's wireless set crackles to life for the first time in hours with a message from the *Princess Sophia*. Leadbetter asked how the ship was faring; Captain Locke wired back that she was taking on water in her forward compartment, but that the ship's engine room, fire room, and aft cargo hold were dry and intact. Although they were still covered with their canvas toppers, Leadbetter noticed that *Princess Sophia*'s lifeboats remain swung out over the sides of her boat deck, ready to be boarded at a moments' notice. One of the *Princess Sophia*'s crew members had also opened her aft shell door on the starboard side of the ship's main deck. Presumably passengers would be off-loaded from this lower point as soon as the weather allowed. *If* the weather allowed. Between the snow and the near-gale-force winds that were whipping the sea into an angry black froth, putting passengers into the boats looks like certain death. "At no time I was there, from the time I saw her, would it have been safe to lower those boats," Captain Leadbetter would later say. "If they had lowered into the water, the sea would either have upset the boat, or she would have punctured on the reef."[15]

Either way Captain Leadbetter cut it, passengers would end up in the bitterly cold water. Hypothermia would take only minutes to set in. For now the safest place they could be seemed to be on the decks of the stranded *Princess Sophia*. He wired Captain Locke, who agreed, and recommended that Leadbetter anchor the *Cedar* until the tide was lower. Locke hoped that the lowering tide would bring better weather and calmer seas.

For the second time that day, the *Cedar* proceeded to her sheltered anchorage. On board the *Princess Sophia*, passengers shuffled back inside the ship's warm public spaces, a handful grumbling as they did so. Since the disaster began they'd been assembled multiple times. Rescue had seemed imminent — even tantalizingly close — for nearly thirty hours. With each passing call to muster that turned out to be a false alarm the message was becoming less and less effective. As he sailed away, Captain Leadbetter wired the *Princess Sophia*:

City of Vancouver Archives AM54-S4-: Bo P434.3.

The engine room on board the *Princess May* illustrates the kind of working environment that engine officers would have had on board the *Princess Sophia*.

AM GOING DROP ANCHOR NEAR SENTINEL ISLAND. WILL BE OUT AGAIN BEFORE DARK. IF WANT ME BEFORE, CALL.[16]

At 1:20 p.m. the *King & Winge* was also forced to seek shelter. Captain James Miller guided his ship approximately five miles from Vanderbilt Reef to Benjamin Island, sheltered by the lee side of Sentinel Island, he dropped anchor at 1:45 p.m. and put his small launch in the water to talk to Captain Leadbetter on the *Cedar*. The two men did not know each other — indeed, at the trial two months later, Captain Miller would refer to Captain Leadbetter as "Captain Lindberg" — but both men would play a very important role in the coming hours.

Captain Miller asked Leadbetter what they should do, and Leadbetter replied that there was nothing the men could do until the weather calmed down. Both men were in agreement about one thing: the *Princess Sophia* had survived a full day up on the reef. A day of being battered by the wind and pounded by the waves, not to mention surviving both high and low tides. If the *Princess Sophia* wasn't firmly wedged atop Vanderbilt Reef, she was certainly doing a good job of fooling everyone.

Captain Miller also recognized another dilemma facing would-be rescuers: even if the storm moderated in the next few hours, they would have the almost impossible task of convincing the passengers and crew of the *Princess Sophia* to abandon their large, seemingly secure ship for a much smaller one bobbing in the sea — and they might have to jump into the sea to do it.

"Judging from the way she looked that morning, if I was on the ship, I don't believe I would have jumped overboard to take a chance in the dorry," said Miller. "The boat looked so safe … judging by the manner [that] she lay there, I didn't think the boat would [ever] come off there."[17]

Instead of obsessing over how to get the passengers off, Miller has a theory bouncing around in his head that might make their temporary home safer: if the *Princess Sophia* were to open her seacocks and let the water flood her double-bottom hull, it would keep the ship firmly rooted to Vanderbilt Reef. That way, if the tide did attempt to wash her off, the weight of the water inside her hull would keep her grounded. It might even stabilize her enough to get the passengers off when the weather let up. It was a risky move though, and the thirty-six-year-old Captain James Miller eventually decided to keep the thought to himself.

On board the *Princess Sophia* the next four hours played out largely as if nothing was wrong at all. Many passengers busied themselves by socializing with one another. Some wrote letters and others — convinced that rescue was imminent despite the worsening weather — began cramming their most valuable personal effects into overcoat pockets as a precaution, in case the worst should happen.

One guest enjoyed semi-privileged status, and during the afternoon he took advantage of this unique position. Juneau Customs Collector John Pugh visited wireless operator David Robinson in his office on the boat deck to ask Robinson to wire a personal message for him. With the *Cedar* anchored and very few messages coming and going, Robinson readily complied. Pugh wired a simple message to his wife in Juneau, intended to reassure her against the news of the disaster that, he assumed, must have made the daily papers. Robinson also took a moment to send out several variations of the same message, "Ship ashore; all safe." Passing them along via the *Cedar*, he first notified his mother before sending similar messages out to relatives of Second Officer Frank Gosse, Third Officer Arthur Murphy, Purser Charles Beadle, and Engineer Charles Waller. Aside from a handful of crew members, Customs Collector Pugh was the only passenger to have a wireless message sent on his behalf.

Outside the weather continued to worsen. As the afternoon progressed even the most optimistic observer could not help but notice that if the ship were to founder rescue would be nearly impossible. Each wave that pounded up against the hull of the ship caused the most violent cacophony of sounds to emanate from deep within her hull. Like an out-of-tune orchestra, it reverberated through every steel plate in her hull, channelling upward before dissipating amongst the atrocious howling noises created by the wind whipping through any gap it could find in the superstructure, from window seals to doors to cargo hatches.

The crew probably didn't share the full extent of their plans with the passengers; more than likely the crew would estimate or offer positive reassurances that the weather would clear up, in time. The line between keeping people informed and creating panic is a thin one. Captain Locke no doubt would have wanted to ensure no one did anything rash — like, perhaps, jump from her decks into the churning sea in a desperate bid to reach shore. Despite that, as the hours dragged on and the situation outside visibly disintegrated before their very eyes, it's likely that the seeds of doubt began to fill the minds of many of the passengers and crew. Visibility outside was evaporating.

The view was replaced by a wall of grey punctuated by speeding flakes of white that swirled around the *Princess Sophia*'s decks. Unable to see more than a few feet outside, cabin fever was probably setting in with the passengers. For the moment, their entire world was confined to the 245-foot *Princess Sophia*.

At 2:00 p.m. *Princess Sophia*'s steam pipe broke again, and the ship was plunged into darkness for the second time in less than a day. In the wireless room, operator David Robinson was absolutely exhausted; he had been awake and at his station ever since the accident occurred the previous morning. Working on his battery set, Robinson messaged Elwood Miller on the *Cedar* to let him know about the power outage. "I told him at that time I was very tired," said Miller. "I had been on for about forty hours … and he said he was tired, too. We made a date to call each other again at 4 p.m. That was about three hours later."[18]

Exhausted, both men lay down in their respective wireless rooms. Miller wore his headphones over his ears and shut his eyes. He never went to sleep, but took a moment to shut the rest of the world from his mind.

On board the *Princess Sophia* darkness was becoming a common theme, enveloping the corridors and public bathrooms and making the ship's interior staterooms on the awning deck impossible to be in for any length of time. Moving between decks was still easy to do; *Princess* Sophia's forward grand staircase was topped with an oversized skylight that illuminated much of the forward parts of the promenade and awning decks. But in less than three hours what little light remained outside would be gone. The thought of spending another evening on the darkened ship, twisting and wrenching in the storm, was probably more than most could bear to think about. Passengers congregated in the observation lounge and smoking room to be near the large picture windows that lined the walls. Some passengers who were lucky enough to have cabins with windows or portholes retreated inside them, eager to be near natural light and out of the ship's darkened interior passageways. Deep within the bowels of the ship, the three-man engineering team worked in near-total darkness to restore the ship's electrical power. The men wished they had the help of First Engineer Archibald Alexander, who had missed the voyage at the last minute to be with his sick children in Victoria.

Around 4:00 p.m., on board the *Cedar*, Captain Leadbetter poked his head into the wireless room to ask operator Elwood Miller if he'd heard from the *Princess Sophia* recently. Miller hadn't, and tried unsuccessfully to raise the ship. Miller didn't think much of the unanswered wire; he told Captain Leadbetter than *Princess Sophia*'s wireless operator, David Robinson, had messaged him a few hours earlier about having a lie-down until conditions moderated. Elwood assumed that Robinson was still sleeping. With the daylight hours quickly drawing to a close, Leadbetter needed to know what the plan of action was. He had wireless operator Miller continue to try to contact the *Princess Sophia*.

Captain James Miller from the *King & Winge* was on board the *Cedar* as Elwood Miller, no relation, tried to hail the *Princess Sophia*. A short message finally came through, around 4:30 p.m., from Captain Locke, stating that everything was all right on board the ship. Miller was swinging his legs over the side of the ship to get into his boat and head back to the *King & Winge* when the message arrived. Captain Leadbetter, looking down at Miller from the deck of the *Cedar*, shrugged and told Miller that Locke said everything was all right on board the stricken ship. It seemed like more of a question than a statement. Leadbetter's black officer's greatcoat was becoming crusted with snow even as he spoke, and the wind whipped painfully at his face.

In his boat, Captain Miller grabbed the oars. He nodded his assent to Leadbetter, agreeing that in all likelihood those aboard the *Princess Sophia* were in no immediate danger, other than the somewhat uncomfortable prospect of having to spend a second night on board the ship as she twisted and groaned on the reef. Neither man said anything else; in all likelihood, with the snow swirling around them and the weather continuing to deteriorate even in their sheltered cove, both were probably uncertain as to what "all right" really meant. With a wave to Captain Leadbetter, Captain Miller began to row himself back to the *King & Winge*. As he did, he could hear the *Cedar*'s cook ring the dinner bell. It echoed off the land around them and reverberated into the growing darkness.

At 4:50 p.m. the wireless waves suddenly crackled with a staccato burst of noise on board the *Cedar*. David Robinson, wireless operator aboard the *Princess Sophia*, was urgently tapping out a message. It was notable for both its brevity and its urgent, pleading tone:

FOR GOD'S SAKE HURRY; WE ARE FOUNDERING ON REEF.[19]

On board the *Cedar*, wireless operator Miller jumped out of his chair and raced to the bridge, where he relayed the message to Captain Leadbetter. "I hauled my anchor up and asked Captain Locke to put some lights out, or sound his whistle, if possible, so as to give me the location of the reef so I could find him," said Leadbetter. "We got no answer that he received that message."[20]

On the *King & Winge*, Captain Miller was just stepping on board when he heard two sharp blasts from the *Cedar's* whistle. He turned his head, but could not see the ship due to the snow and fog. *Why is she raising her anchors?* he wondered.

Her anchor had barely cleared the water's surface when the *Cedar* began to move forward. Captain Leadbetter brought his ship alongside the *King & Winge* and asked them via megaphone to begin manoeuvring to the wreck as soon as the weather allowed. It was a startling turn of events from the conversation the two captains had shared barely twenty minutes earlier. On the deck of the *King & Winge*, Captain Miller replied that he would relieve the *Cedar* in one hour. With the storm intensifying by the minute, neither of the men could afford to take any chances.

Half an hour had passed since they received the initial SOS from the *Princess Sophia*, and Captain Leadbetter drove his ship full speed through the worsening storm, which had turned into a full-on blizzard. The heavy seas were making it difficult to keep the *Cedar* on a straight course. Snow obscured Leadbetter's view as it raced across the windows of his wheelhouse. Although he was steaming past Sentinel Island as quickly as he could, Leadbetter himself would later admit that the storm was already wreaking havoc. "It was impossible to hear the fog signal on Sentinel Island," he would later say, "or see the light."[21] The experienced mariner guessed he was between five hundred yards (an eighth of a mile) off the island, but had no way of knowing for sure. At that moment he couldn't even see the bow. Still, he commanded his ship on through the night. "I could not tell or state just how far we had run, or what my position was, and I could not see anything or hear anything."[22]

At 5:20 p.m., another frantic message came from the *Princess Sophia*:

FOR GOD'S SAKE HURRY, THE WATER IS COMING INTO MY ROOM.[23]

There was more to the message, but it was garbled and cut off. Tossed around by the heavy seas, Elwood Miller tapped away at his key in the wireless room on board the *Cedar*, reassuring Robinson on the *Princess Sophia* that they were coming to their aid. "I talked to the operator for a few minutes on his battery until it went weak," Miller would later say. "I told him not to say anything more, only what was absolutely necessary, and to save his battery."[24] A weak, garbled signal came back from the *Princess Sophia*:

ALRIGHT, I WILL, BUT YOU TALK TO ME SO I KNOW YOU ARE COMING.[25]

For such a simple message, it carried a tremendous amount of weight. Elwood Miller could practically taste David Robinson's fear. Miller quickly responded, once again assuring the *Princess Sophia's* wireless operator that they were steaming to the scene as fast as they could.

He waited for a response. It never came.

CHAPTER NINE
BEACHING THE *STAR PRINCESS*

0143 HRS, JUNE 23, 1995
ON BOARD *STAR PRINCESS* IN LYNN CANAL,
NEAR POUNDSTONE ROCK

Asleep in his berth, Relief Alaska State Pilot Ronald Kutz was jolted awake at 01:42. He felt the floor of his stateroom shake and rattle, almost as if the ship had struck a rogue wave. Realizing something was amiss, he sat up in bed and quickly dressed. In mere minutes he stepped out of his stateroom door into the brightly lit corridor. Running on adrenaline, he made his way to the navigation bridge.

Pilot Kutz wasn't alone. The grounding had awakened *Star Princess*'s master, Emanuele Chiesa, along with the other deck officers, the chief engineer, and the assistant engineer. Captain Chiesa immediately emerged onto the bridge, where Pilot Nerup informed him that the vessel had struck Poundstone Rock. Without being told to, the chief engineer and assistant engineer simultaneously made their way to the engine room to await further orders, in keeping with the emergency procedures that have been established by Princess Cruises.

Captain Chiesa quickly assessed the situation. During the minutes immediately following the collision, *Star Princess* had lost a substantial portion of her forward momentum. Dropping to a speed of just barely 3.5 knots, the ship had also run off course and was drifting on a heading of 150°T. Following orders, the helmsman immediately brought the ship around to 155°T to straighten her out, and her speed was doubled. Propellers churning in the ink-black water, the *Star Princess* slowly increased her speed to 7.6 knots.

At 01:43 Pilot Nerup radioed the United States Coast Guard to advise them of the grounding. Less than a minute later, the *Fair Princess* finally passed the *Star Princess* on her port side. *Fair Princess* was roughly half a mile off the *Star Princess*, but no one on the bridge team seemed to care. Instead, Captain Chiesa asked off-duty Pilot Ronald J. Kutz where the *Star Princess* could be beached to prevent her from sinking.

It fell to the off-duty Pilot Kutz to deliver the crushing blow: the water in that part of Lynn Canal was too deep to beach the ship. Instead, Kutz recommended that

Captain Chiesa sail for Auke Bay — some fourteen miles to the southeast of Poundstone Rock. There, she would be sheltered from any weather that should develop, and the shallow waters should prevent the vessel from foundering.

With the decision to head to Auke Bay made, Captain Chiesa asked the staff captain to go sound the ship. The staff captain did so and reported that the ship was not taking on any water. Because of the force of the collision, Captain Chiesa was doubtful. He had the staff captain make a second, more thorough, inspection. This time, the report that came back was far from good: seawater was entering the ship's double hull on the starboard side. Four tanks were flooding, and the ship's starboard propeller shaft was losing lubrication oil.

If he needed it, Captain Chiesa had plenty of help in the area. Within a fifteen-mile radius were five other cruise ships, including the *Fair Princess*, *Glacier Bay Explorer*, *Golden Princess*, *Universe Explorer*, and Norwegian Cruise Line's *Windward*. Preferring to call on a company ship, Captain Chiesa radioed the *Golden Princess* and asked if they could come and rendezvous with his stricken vessel. Sailing south of the *Star Princess* on a northbound course, the *Golden Princess* agreed to meet up with *Star Princess* as soon as possible.

At the same time, the first officer aboard *Star Princess* had determined that while the ship had taken on enough seawater to increase her draught by five inches she was not in any immediate danger of sinking. He reported his findings to Captain Chiesa, who made an announcement over the crew public address system at 01:55 to inform them of the situation.

The master's message was stern but clear: the ship had hit an obstruction in the water, but the situation was not all that serious. Still, he advised the crew to remain calm and at the ready, and he urged them to stay awake in order to listen for further updates on the condition of the vessel.

He also imparted one final piece of information: while the vast majority of the *Star Princess* passengers were asleep, a few remained up in the ship's public rooms and lounges. Captain Chiesa told the crew that if they encountered any guests up and about, they were to quietly advise them of the current situation.[1] Not wanting to unnecessarily alarm the guests with a situation he felt he had under control, Captain Chiesa decided not to make any announcements over the passenger public address system, nor did he activate the general emergency alarm. He was concerned that any announcement made shortly before two in the morning would unnecessarily alarm his passengers.[2] With the ship's stability no longer in question and the *Star Princess* steaming for Auke Bay, Captain Chisea chose to keep his guests blissfully unaware.

Still, Captain Chisea decided to prepare for any and all eventualities. To that end, he immediately ordered that the ship's lifeboats be readied for possible launching. This involved swinging them out on their hydraulic davits and lowering them down to the promenade deck for possible embarkation. Captain Chisea knew each of the Schat-Harding lifeboats could accommodate one hundred and fifty guests apiece. Together with all the lifesaving apparatus on board, that was more than enough for every single passenger and crew member — if it came to that.

Meanwhile, the officers on the bridge of *Star Princess* busied themselves with administrative work necessitated by the change of plans. Captain Chiesa requested and received permission from authorities in Juneau to proceed into Auke Bay. While the process had been greatly expedited, the navigation bridge was a flurry of activity. Every senior officer was awake and at their designated command post. Commands were being issued, phone calls made, faxes sent and received. What had been a serene wheelhouse just moments earlier became a crowded beehive of activity.

Curiously absent from these proceedings was Alaska State Pilot Robert K. Nerup. The man who was largely responsible for the grounding faded into obscurity during the ensuing barrage of orders. His trust evaporated, Nerup went nearly unnoticed by every senior officer for the next several hours. At 02:30, a little over forty-five minutes after the collision, he was relieved by Pilot Ronald J. Kutz. Kutz had navigated in Auke Bay before; Robert Nerup had not.

During the next hour, *Star Princess* sailed silently through the night. To the casual observer on deck, it would have only appeared as though the ship were sailing slightly slower than normal. Her deck lights still burned brightly and her passengers were, for the most part, asleep. In fact, the only sign of anything out of the ordinary was the lights of the *Golden Princess*, which were just visible in the distance off the side of the ship.

At 03:30 *Star Princess* entered Auke Bay harbour. Located north of Juneau, not far from Juneau International Airport, Auke Bay is a sleepy little town that contains a handful of shops and restaurants, a single school, and the prerequisite church. Cruise ships of any size sailing into the harbour are an uncommon sight, but ships the size of *Star Princess* are positively unheard of. The only craft regularly seen are pleasure boats and the blue-and-white hulls of the Alaska State Ferries that tie up at the nearby terminal. The town's residents would awake in a few hours to find their lazy seaside view had changed somewhat during the night.

The sound of her anchors shattering the stillness of the night, *Star Princess* finally came to a stop in Auke Bay nearly two hours after the accident had occurred. The ship was still afloat, and Captain Chiesa allowed himself a small sigh of relief that they had reached Auke Bay and the relative safety of Juneau. Passengers would have to be offloaded and put up in hotels in Juneau — or even flown home — that much was clear. What remained unknown was exactly how much damage had been done to the ship's hull. Clearly there had been a breach. The question was: how bad?

At 04:37 the first underwater dive teams approached the *Star Princess*. Over the next two hours, until nearly seven in the morning, they meticulously inspected every inch of the hull from stem to stern. The prognosis was clear: *Star Princess* could be repaired, but she'd need to go into dry dock for more permanent repairs. That meant disembarking her current passengers and finding a suitable (and available) dry dock space farther south, either in Esquimalt, Vancouver, Seattle, or Portland.

The damage to the hull was extensive. Both the keel and the double-bottomed hull had been impacted, the latter of which has suffered two tears from Poundstone Rock, each measuring eight inches wide and up to one hundred feet long, on the starboard side of the ship. Damage to the inner hull ran mainly along the centreline of the ship. Poundstone

Night falls on Juneau. *Star Princess* was bound here in 1995, destined to tie up at the docks at centre.

Rock evidently scraped and bounced its way along the length of the ship: blades from the ship's starboard propeller sustained damage significant enough for them to need to be replaced. *Star Princess* carried a spare set of blades that could be attached, but the damage to the rest of the hull was so extensive that they could only be fitted once the ship arrived in dry dock. In all, twenty-two fuel tanks, ballast tanks, and cofferdams were damaged. There was also evidence that she had been leaking oil from her damaged fuel tanks, and within hours a containment boom was set up around her hull. A total of twenty litres, or five gallons, mixed in with the waters of Lynn Canal near Poundstone Rock.

As the morning went on, passengers awoke to discover that the ship was not in Juneau as they had expected. Instead, they were nestled in a small cove with just a few buildings visible off in the distance. Unless they had visited Alaska before, few likely knew they were just a few miles north of Juneau. Here Captain Chiesa made a curious decision: despite the fact that regular services like breakfast began around six in the morning, he waited until 9:18 a.m. to broadcast an announcement over the ship's public address system.[3] Nearly eight hours after the accident with Poundstone Rock, passengers learned of the situation on board — and that their voyage had come to an abrupt halt. Captain Chiesa knew that getting 1,568 passengers and their luggage off the vessel in a bay without an actual dock would be a challenge. Though he didn't tell them this, it would take two full days to disembark every guest on board the *Star Princess* using the ship's own tender boats and private launches.

For the foreseeable future, the *Star Princess*'s 1995 season in Alaska had come to an unexpected close. On the evening of June 27, 1995, *Star Princess* raised her anchors and sailed without any guests out into the Pacific Ocean, bound for the shipyards in Portland, Oregon. She would not return to Alaska for nearly two months.

CHAPTER TEN
THOSE LAST MINUTES
– PRINCESS SOPHIA

5:20 P.M., FRIDAY, OCTOBER 25, 1918
ABOARD *PRINCESS SOPHIA* ON VANDERBILT REEF, ALASKA

FOR GOD'S SAKE HURRY, THE WATER IS COMING INTO MY ROOM.[1]

What happened in those final minutes aboard the *Princess Sophia* is anyone's guess. Divers would later discover many of the victims clustered in the ship's social hall, forward of the main staircase. Each wore their lifebelt, suspending them in one final dance, forever frozen in time. In fact, most who were recovered from inside the wreck were wearing their lifebelts. If orders hadn't explicitly been given by Captain Locke, passengers took it upon themselves in their final moments to affix their lifebelts and gather their personal belongings.

Some passengers were gathered in the ship's public spaces when the end came. In the observation lounge Louise Davis stood alone while chaos ensued around her. A few either retreated to their staterooms, or were simply caught off guard and never had a chance to escape the rushing water as *Princess Sophia* slipped stern-first off Vanderbilt Reef. In Cabin 35 Sarah O'Brien was in the midst of comforting Ilene Winchell, who was travelling alone, when the ship shuddered violently and began her plunge.

Here, even as this end-game played out to its horrifying conclusion, order and purpose seem to have escaped Captain Locke. Passengers and crew were literally swarming the decks of the *Princess Sophia*, both inside and out, during her final moments afloat. There was, it seemed, no organized effort to abandon ship. People were scattered all over, in staterooms, public rooms, and the open decks. Passengers were even found, fully clothed, in the public bathrooms. Even if the ship were to have foundered exactly after the last message tapped out by David Robinson, a full half hour had elapsed between his first and last message. Yet most victims were found with their watches frozen at 6:50 p.m. ship's time; 5:50 p.m. Alaskan time. This gave Captain Locke a full hour to order an evacuation. Most signs indicate that never happened.

As the ship went down, passengers took matters into their own hands: from the decks of the *Princess Sophia*, clad in their lifebelts and warm coats, and carrying many of their valuables in their pockets, they clambered over the deck railings and jumped into the water. But there, too, death was waiting. Survival in the frigid, swirling seas already bordered on impossible, but the 1,933 barrels of thick, heavy bunker oil that poured from the ship's fuel tanks as she went down made death a certainty. A few grades above raw sludge, the bunker oil coated those who jumped into the water, clinging to their bodies like tar and sapping the buoyancy of their lifebelts. Shocked into taking a deep breath when they first entered the icy water, it filled their lungs and, mercifully, ceased their struggle.

The screaming of passengers and the horrifying protests of the ship herself emanated from Vanderbilt Reef, only to be drowned out by the howling wind and fierce snow. To the *Cedar*, steaming to the rescue, the *Princess Sophia* was all but invisible. Captain Leadbetter drove his ship hard through the raging blizzard. She pitched and rolled in the heavy seas, but Leadbetter didn't give an inch. He remained in the wheelhouse, legs spread apart to keep his balance amidst the rolling deck, eyes focused on the grey in front of him. Simply keeping his ship on course was a hellish task. "I ran full speed toward the *Princess Sophia* until 5:55 p.m.," he would later say. "While I was out searching for the *Sophia* that night, we got into communication with the steamer *Atlas*, and I wired the captain where I was, and what I was doing, and relayed the message from the *Sophia* … She [*Atlas*] was 46 miles from the wreck, feeling her way in a blinding snowstorm for anchorage in Taku Harbor."[2]

Blinded by the snow and the darkness that had descended upon his ship, Captain Leadbetter continued to search in vain for the *Princess Sophia*; a ship that to him seemed to have literally disappeared. Hidden by the fog and obscured by the snow, he was spared the sight of the petite Canadian Pacific ship's final death throes.

Once her bottom had been torn away by the reef, water rushed in to the *Princess Sophia*'s engine room, flooding the machinery spaces and causing her boilers to violently explode. Portholes shattered under the increased pressure being put on them by the ship's hull, and the entire midships deck structure buckled under the weight. Steam blew out through the ship's funnel, pulverizing it instantly and sending hot clouds of air, soot, and ash firing into the night sky. As the ship twisted and groaned on her descent into the ocean, water poured in through the broken portholes, hastening the inevitable. It quickly spread to the oversized cargo hold spaces, engulfing the twenty-five horses that filled the ship with their cries of protest. Old Billy, the horse belonging to Walter Barnes, was among them. Given how close Barnes was to his trusted old friend, in all likelihood the old prospector was caught up in the hold trying to free Old Billy, or on his way down to the holds when the *Princess Sophia* began her final plunge.

Racing up through the machinery spaces, stairwells, and ventilation ducts aboard the *Princess Sophia*, the cold, black ocean finally engulfed the brightly polished woodwork of her passenger interiors. It sped along her corridors and seeped into her staterooms, travelling from the aft of the ship forward. It swirled around her grand forward staircase and swept away those guests and crew who had gathered in the social hall. As *Princess Sophia*'s list became more apparent, anything not bolted down crashed aft, down her decks, as she began her journey to the bottom. With the ocean rapidly taking up space in the interior of the ship, windows began to blow out as the air pressure inside became too great for the glass panes to handle.

Up on the boat deck, wireless operator David Robinson was likely swept up by the oil-coated sea as he tried to save himself. The windows of the officer's quarters were blown out at some point, along with those in the wheelhouse. Though it is unknown where Captain Locke was on the ship during her final moments, it seems likely he was in or near the wheelhouse when the end came. He, like so many others on board in those last few minutes, probably tried to picture his family before the waters rushed up to greet him.

Prior to the sinking the doors to the wheelhouse had been opened and placed in their latch-pin hooks, securing them to the sides of the deck house as if it were a hot summer's day. As the water swept past the officer's quarters and engulfed the wheelhouse, it took with it *Princess Sophia*'s charts, navigational warnings, and the ship's log book. Aided by the heavy bunker oil coating everything in its path, Mother Nature succeeded in covering her own tracks; the ship's log book was never recovered.

In a last-ditch effort to save themselves, those passengers and crew who had not already jumped or were trapped below decks tried to get away in *Princess Sophia*'s lifeboats. Most were caught in the falls still attached to the ship's davits, and were dragged down as the ship went under. Of the few boats that managed to get away in the final seconds, nearly all were pulverized against Vanderbilt Reef by the storm that raged on unabated. A few passengers and crew latched onto the complicated and ineffective approved buoyancy apparatuses that had been lashed to the roof of the officer's quarters. As they floated free, passengers struggling in the water frantically tied themselves to them in order to stay afloat; an act that merely bought them minutes, if not seconds, in the freezing, oil-coated water.

One boat, however, did manage to reach shore. One of *Princess Sophia*'s eight steel lifeboats was found washed ashore on a rocky beach. Those who found the lifeboat first claimed to have seen footprints in the snow leading away from it, and the body of Second Officer Frank Gosse was discovered not far away. Covered in his officer's greatcoat, he was found frozen to death, with a bad gash to his head. The connect-the-dots logic was that Second Officer Gosse had made it to shore in the washed-up lifeboat and had set out to find help before succumbing to the cold, his injuries, or both. In an article in the *Dawson Daily News* published nearly two months later, Juneau's Special Deputy Collector of Customs C.D. Garfield would dispute that these tracks were ever made by Gosse. Sadly, how Gosse came to be on shore didn't truly matter; he did not live to tell the tale of what had occurred during *Princess Sophia*'s final moments.

There would be no outside witnesses to the sinking, either. At the very moment the *Princess Sophia* foundered the storm seemed to redouble its efforts, intensifying with frightening

The captain of the *Princess Adelaide*, a sister ship to the *Princess Sophia*, enters a notation in the ship's log book in this 1941 photo. Captain Locke and his officers would have had a similar setup. The *Princess Sophia*'s log books were never found.

speed. Aboard the *Cedar*, Captain Leadbetter was forced to turn his ship around and seek shelter. Repeatedly sounding the ship's whistle, Leadbetter gingerly felt his way back through the canal to his anchorage. His mind never left the stricken Canadian Pacific vessel, though. After reaching shelter, he informed his crew that there was still work to be done. "I left orders to call me as soon as the weather cleared so that I could find the wreck," he would later say.[3]

By six o'clock in the evening of Friday, October 25, 1918, all that remained of the Canadian Pacific Steamship *Princess Sophia* was her forward mast. Submerged up to the masthead running light, it rose out of the water like a tombstone.

When help finally arrived at daybreak the following morning, the light would be the only sign that anything out of the ordinary had ever occurred here at all. Even Captain Leadbetter was shocked by the calm scene that confronted him in the early morning hours. "There was no sign of any survivors at all," he would recall. "No sign of the wreck, any flotage [sic] at all, until we reached the northwest end of Shelter Island. There were three overturned lifeboats about one mile south of the narrows."[4] For the crew of the *Cedar*, the full horror of that day would linger in their memories and nightmares for years to come.

The most horrible twist of fate, though, was delivered by Mother Nature herself. Just twelve hours after the *Princess Sophia* had foundered, the snow, wind, and heavy seas that had battered her for nearly three consecutive days suddenly subsided.

CHAPTER ELEVEN
AFTERMATH
– CHAOS AND CONFUSION

We lost our battle with the elements, and there were no survivors to tell the tale.

– Wireless message from *Cedar* [1]

By daybreak on Saturday, October 26, 1918, Captain John Leadbetter confirmed the worst had happened to the *Princess Sophia*. As he gingerly manoeuvred the Lighthouse Tender *Cedar* near Vanderbilt reef, he could see no sign of the stricken Canadian Pacific vessel. It was still snowing heavily, though the dangerous swells and fearsome winds of the night before had subsided. Peering through the windows of the wheelhouse, he strained to see much beyond his own bow. He held out hope that, somehow, he might spot the *Princess Sophia*'s white lifeboats bobbing nearby, filled with survivors. Gradually, out of the haze and snow ahead of him, he began to make out a solitary object. It looked like a tree branch suspended vertically in the water. Confusion, however, quickly gave way to recognition: the object sticking out of the water was no branch. It was *Princess Sophia*'s forward mast, submerged nearly to the white running light affixed three quarters of the way up.

At 9:15 a.m., the *Cedar* broke the news to Frank Lowle, Canadian Pacific's tireless Juneau agent. In his telegram, Captain Leadbetter stated there were no survivors, but that he would continue to cruise Lynn Canal in the hopes of finding someone. It was a task that would turn out to be more horrifying than anyone had likely imagined. Thanks to the strong winds and swells of the previous night, and the enormous tidal fluctuations in the area, the *Cedar*, assisted by the *King & Winge* and other boats, searched for three hours before finding a single body. Most of those found on the surface were strapped into their lifebelts and coated in the thick bunker oil that had gushed from the ship as she went down.

Despite the fact that the *Princess Sophia* was obviously no longer on Vanderbilt Reef, and unquestionably sank, it wasn't until 11:30 a.m. that the first evidence of the ship's foundering was located: a solitary white metal lifeboat had washed ashore, and lay overturned on Shelter Island. Lookouts positioned aboard the *King & Winge* had spotted it, and the order was given to put the ship's smaller boats in the water to make a closer inspection. As the crew aboard the *King & Winge* were doing so, Captain Leadbetter spotted three white lifeboats resting on shore and sent Second Officer Robert Martin to examine them. Arriving on the beach, Martin quickly determined there were no survivors to be found. The only thing he found was the skylight that once sat atop the *Princess Sophia*'s forward staircase; it had broken off during the sinking and was lying on the beach, next to the three boats.

Nearly eighteen hours after the *Princess Sophia* slid off Vanderbilt reef to her icy grave, the first body was spotted. Then another. Then another. The corpses that had refused to present themselves all morning were suddenly at every turn, and nearly every ship on the scene was stopping to pluck bodies from the waters of Lynn Canal before the tides returned to performing their gruesome work. Though no one was aware of it at the time, retrieving the bodies of the 343 passengers and crew aboard the *Princess Sophia* would stretch on for months. Some were simply never found.

One of those to disappear seemingly without a trace was *Princess Sophia*'s captain, Leonard Locke. Though the bodies of many of his senior officers and junior deckhands were found in the coming days and weeks, Locke's body was never recovered from the surface or the wreckage.

In Juneau, Canadian Pacific Agent Frank Lowle was devastated by the telegram he received from the *Cedar* early that morning. Like everyone else, Lowle had become accustomed to receiving a steady, even monotonous, stream of news from the *Princess Sophia* that was essentially variations on the "still stuck, all well" theme. Lowle cancelled the Juneau hotel arrangements he had spent so much of the previous day arranging. Wearily, he turned all his resources to the grim task of recovering bodies. Before he did anything, though, he wired Captain Troup in Victoria with the unthinkable news.

Even then, at this late stage in the disaster, word still didn't filter down to Captain Troup in Victoria until late in the afternoon. At 3:38 p.m. he received Frank Lowle's message stating that the ship had been lost, and there were no survivors. Troup immediately ordered Lowle to put rescue efforts into play, and to continue to search for any survivors who might have gotten off in the boats or made it to shore. Thanks to the unpredictable nature of wireless communications at the time, Captain Troup had no way of knowing that his dependable Juneau agent had been doing that very thing for the past six hours. Through no fault of his own, the head of Canadian Pacific's coastal fleet division was still the last man to learn of developments in Alaska. Professionally, he'd committed to the grim task at hand. Personally, the *Princess Sophia* left Captain Troup a shattered man. At the official inquiries in Canada and the United States, he was called on to testify to everything that transpired after the *Princess Sophia* left Skagway. He was forced to endure long hours of inane questioning that ran the gamut from sensationalistic (Did Captain Locke entertain young female passengers in his cabin? *No*) to the absurd (Was there any incompetence on the part of Frank Lowle due to the delays in passing the wireless messages along? *No*).

The inanity of the questions at the inquiry weren't entirely without merit. On November 4, less than two weeks after the sinking, the small Canadian Pacific

Steamship known as the *Tees* quietly steamed up Lynn Canal, anchoring not far from Vanderbilt Reef. Aboard the 1893-built vessel were two divers, John Donaldson and Thomas Veitch, along with their employer, Superintendent T.W. Allan of the Pacific Salvage Company in Victoria. Joined by a supply ship called the *Santa Rita*, which contained two sets of diving gear, both vessels arrived on the scene just after 8:30 in the morning.

Diver Donaldson went into the icy waters first. He initially found the seas quite calm, but was quickly caught up in strong underwater currents as he passed sixty feet of depth. The condition of the wreck was also proving hazardous to his long-term health; rigging and wiring were strewn about, and jagged metal protruded from the areas of the wreck that had torn free during the sinking. Donaldson managed to plant his feet on the forward open deck, where he found a single body, which he brought to the surface. It was fifty-two-year-old George Paddock, of Dawson City. The jack of all trades had family that he had left behind in New York State, and Paddock was returning home to be with his daughter, who had fallen ill.

Donaldson's main objective, however, wasn't recovering bodies. Despite the fact that hundreds of passengers were still missing, the Pacific Salvage Company had been hired to assess whether salvaging the wreck of the *Princess Sophia* was even possible. They had also been engaged to recover a single very important piece of cargo: the Wells-Fargo safe that had been loaded onto the ship in Skagway at the last moment.

Once the body of Paddock had been successfully taken aboard the *Tees*, and before diving back down to the wreck, Donaldson told his boss, T.W. Allan, that the strong currents were preventing him from going farther aft than the ship's wheelhouse. Allan persuaded him to give it another try, and the dutiful employee once again submerged beneath the inky waves. Once again Donaldson was no match for the current, which was now so strong and murky that he could no longer make out any details of the wreck aft of the wheelhouse. Increasingly concerned that he was going to tangle his suit on wreckage he couldn't see — or that he could be simply swept away by the current — Donaldson returned to the *Tees* to swap places with his colleague, Diver Thomas Veitch.

Veitch also found the conditions on the wreck less than ideal for making a complete survey of the ship. Instead, he was lowered into *Princess Sophia*'s forward cargo hold, where he found and attached a line to the Wells-Fargo safe. Shortly after lunchtime on November 4, 1918, the safe broke the surface of the increasingly choppy waters and was loaded onto the *Santa Rita*. Inside was $62,000 in gold bullion.

Having achieved one of their objectives, the *Tees* and the *Santa Rita* left Vanderbilt Reef and the grave of the *Princess Sophia* shortly after one in the afternoon.

Four days later, on November 8th — exactly two weeks to the day of the sinking — the three men were back at Vanderbilt Reef for another shot at determining whether or not the *Princess Sophia* could be salvaged. This time, divers Donaldson and Veitch both went down to the wreck together, with Veitch leading and Donaldson serving as a guide for his air hose. Once again, the strong currents sweeping past the wreckage created a perilous atmosphere. The two men were able to gingerly pick their way through the wreckage to the chart room just aft of the wheelhouse. The room looked like a disaster zone: Donaldson and Veitch found that the wooden floor had been entirely swept away, along with much of its contents. All that remained were three bags of mail that had become tangled up in one another; two were resting on the small chunk of flooring that remained while the third dangled precariously over the black void.

The sacks of mail were retrieved and brought to the surface. Interestingly, they carry no letters of any kind, having been filled instead by $70,000 in gold. This "mail" was placed in T.W. Allan's room aboard the *Tees* for safekeeping, and delivered to Victoria personally. Where they went after that is unknown.

By ten in the morning of November 8, less than four hours after having arrived on the scene, the weather turned so ugly that both ships were once again forced to seek shelter. The Wells-Fargo safe, three sacks of mail and gold, and a single body were all the men had to show for two days of work.

The actions and motives of T.W. Allan, John Davidson, and Thomas Veitch would be scrutinized in the coming months, with the investigation in the United States going so far as to accuse Allan of either destroying or tampering with the ship's log books, which were never recovered anyway. If Allan is genuine in his testimony — there's little reason in either his background or character to believe he wouldn't be — then they were likely washed away when the chart-room floor collapsed during the sinking. Still, during the American investigation Allan claimed that Canadian Pacific had given them no specific directives regarding the recovery of the Wells-Fargo safe. This statement seems highly implausible, particularly considering how strong the current was around the wreck at the time. Divers with no knowledge of the ship's general arrangement, layout, or storage spaces would have had to search for days to locate the safe; T.W. Allan's Pacific Salvage Company managed to not only locate but also retrieve the safe on the very first trip down to the wreck. That same selective amnesia would dog Allan when the question of the mail sacks and their $70,000 payday surfaced during the American inquiry three years later. Allan naively claimed to have never opened the sacks to check on their contents.

Similar accusations, whether founded or not, would surface on both sides of the border, as investigators and prosecutors sought to establish liability and even negligence on the part of the Canadian Pacific Steamship Company, their subsidiaries, suppliers, and employees for their role in the sinking.

In his journal, Alaskan Governor Thomas J. Riggs, Jr., would put a face to a more human side of the disaster. While preparations were being made to dive to the wreck for salvage purposes, Governor Riggs took time on November 2, 1918, to visit the morgue in Juneau.

I went to the morgue today. All these poor silent bodies stretched out and the embalmers from all the towns working over the corpses. There are 179 recovered so far. I do not think there will be very many more found as the recent storms have scattered them far and wide.[2]

Canadian Pacific's Juneau agent, Frank Lowle, also suffered through a grim and unenviable task in early November. "My length of service in Alaska came in useful in helping me to recognize, or know of, fully 60% of bodies recovered," he would later write. "[One hundred and eighty-two] bodies are recovered to-date … we were all near the breaking point so that if many more had come in at that time, I fear things would have been very serious."[3]

However downplayed in his letter, the obvious mental strain on Frank Lowle spilled from his note, which he wrote to Captain James Troupe in Victoria as a detailed account of his actions from the first distress signal to the grisly aftermath.

Nakedly, Lowle closed his letter with a sentence filled with sadness and regret. "I trust it will not be yours or my lot to experience a similar sad and overwhelming disaster. Quite half of those lost are personal friends."[4]

Lowle wasn't alone in his feelings; in Juneau, Skagway, and points farther north, nearly every citizen was either directly or indirectly affected by the sinking. Those who were fortunate enough to not lose family, friends, or loved ones quite often knew someone who had. Even in the much-larger cities of Vancouver and Victoria the sinking of the *Princess Sophia* had cut deeply, particularly for those who worked aboard other Canadian Pacific steamships.

One of the saddest post-sinking events to play out occurred that December. Al Winchell, who lost his wife, Ilene, in the sinking, hired Juneau diver Selmer Jacobson to search the wreckage for her remains. Ilene had battled with frequent premonitions of her death in the days leading up to her trip south, and she had made Al promise to find her remains and bury her next to her mother if anything should happen to her. Al Winchell spent his last dime to fulfill his wife's last wish.

Suiting up, Selmer Jacobson dropped into the frigid waters above the wreck just after two in the afternoon on December 21. The upper decks of the *Princess Sophia* were a tangled mess of twisted metal and blown-out windows, so Jacobson made his way along the main deck to the forward hatch, fighting the powerful currents as he did so. Upon entering the wreck, he immediately encountered the body of a man resting on the deck. A grim scene awaited him as he swam farther in: enormous legs hung suspended in space, drifting toward him with the current. They belonged to the horses the *Princess Sophia* had embarked in Skagway.

In the observation lounge on promenade deck, Jacobson found the body of a woman floating near the ceiling. It was Louise Davis. Her husband, twenty-five-year-old Richard Harding Davis, was apparently separated from her when the end came.

Jacobson next made his way to the ship's wheelhouse, which was mainly intact except for some shattered windows. However, he discovered that the strong currents had swept everything out of the room; not even a log book or a stray navigational instrument remained inside. There was also no one to be found.

The officer's quarters just aft of the bridge hadn't fared nearly as well. Their ceiling had been blown out, taking with it the skylight that the *Cedar*'s Second Officer Robert Martin had found washed ashore on the beach nearly two months earlier. "It appears to me," Jacobson would later say, "that the smokestack has broke aft, about six feet aft of the [deck] house, and has fell forward and broke into those rooms."[5]

Jacobson could see clothing floating around inside the remains of the officer's quarters. But diving in 1918 was an inexact science at best, compounded by the late hour of the day. With daylight fading and darkness approaching, Jacobson made his way to the surface around four that afternoon, hoping to make another go of it the following day. Beset by the miserable December weather, Jacobson had to wait several days before conditions improved enough to allow him to continue his search for Ilene Winchell.

When he finally got back to the wreck — once again, late in the afternoon and with daylight fading — Selmer Jacobson peered into the stateroom windows on the starboard side of the vessel, but could see no evidence of bodies. "I went through approximately all of the ship," he would testify. "All of the rooms on the starboard side of it — all of the rooms which I could view from the outside; there was a couple of those staterooms, inside rooms, and I don't know what they contained, but the outside rooms on the starboard side to the best of my knowledge contained no bodies."[6]

Making his way past the superstructure to the adjacent smoking room in the deck house situated at the stern of the promenade deck, Jacobson peered through the windows, but couldn't see anyone. A quick swim inside confirmed his initial thoughts: the room was completely deserted. Before leaving, he paused long enough to take the name plates off the door to the smoking room.

From the smoking room Jacobson made his way to Stateroom 35 on the aft port side of the ship's awning deck. In conversations with Canadian Pacific, Al Winchell learned that Ilene was given Stateroom 35. Jacobson found the room, but there were two women inside instead of the solo traveller he was expecting to find.

"I went to Room No. 35, which is a little aft of the smokestack on the port side, and there was two ladies in that room," he testified. "One had a life preserver on, on the floor, under the ceiling. The other one, her hair was entwined in the window and I could feel what I presumed was her head under the bed pillow."[7]

But Jacobson was unable to retrieve the two women because the stateroom window had separated. Despite having broken the glass panes to gain entry to the room, the wooden sash supporting the two-piece window refused to budge. Jacobson had to return with a saw on a different day to cut the window's wooden sash open. With the sash removed, he was able to recover the body of the woman in the life preserver. After being brought to the surface, the body was determined to be that of Sarah O'Brien, who was travelling on board the *Princess Sophia* with her husband, William, and their five children. At the time of her identification it was assumed that O'Brien went to Ilene Winchell's stateroom to comfort her during the sinking, and that the two women had become trapped as the ship slid off the reef. Identifying Winchell, however, would prove to be a difficult task: the body of the woman Jacobson spotted lying on the bed with her hair caught in the window was nowhere to be found. Jacobson surmised the strong current swirling around in the room when he broke the glass panes of the window had picked her up and washed her remains out of the wreckage.

Although he may have been initially hired by Al Winchell, Selmer Jacobson's testimony revealed that Canadian Pacific stepped up to the plate once he discovered more bodies. In all, the Juneau diver had made five separate trips out to the wreck, but questioned how much more he could do to help recover the remains of those still trapped within the sunken ship. Testifying at the inquiry in early 1919, Jacobson admitted "I don't see that I can do any more. The bodies is getting in such a state now … it is getting pretty creepy, to tell you the truth, Your Honor."[8] He still thought that more bodies could be found if a thorough interior search of the vessel was done, but Jacobson didn't do it because he was diving alone and was concerned about becoming trapped in the ship's interior passageways and corridors.

For Al Winchell, mentally exhausted and financially drained by repeated failures to find the remains of his wife, closure would not come until July 1919 when, after a series of false starts, the body of his beloved wife was finally pulled from the wreckage. History doesn't record where in the ship she was found. Though he honoured his promise, burying Ilene's remains in San Francisco near her mother, he was never the same again. After having mounted a relentless nine-month search for his wife, Al Winchell, much like the *Princess Sophia* herself, rapidly sank into obscurity.

Perhaps nothing helped to sweep the *Princess Sophia* from the front pages of the newspapers more than the events of November 11, 1918. Just seventeen days after the *Princess Sophia* carried her passengers and crew to their watery grave in Alaska, the Great War officially came to a close on the eleventh hour of the eleventh day of the eleventh month. Victory in Europe was a major cause for celebration. The global conflict had dragged on for over four years, and had so many casualties that it had been called "The War to End All Wars." In that short time over thirty-seven million people worldwide had been killed; a number that encompassed more than half the total number of enlisted troops around the globe. Victory, particularly on this unimaginable scale, overshadowed failure. The sinking of the *Princess Sophia* quickly became a footnote in history, relegated to the margins of a few west coast newspapers — mainly publications like the *Dawson Daily News, Victoria Daily Colonist*, and the *Vancouver Sun* that would have had a more personal connection with the victims. Unlike the sinking of the *Titanic* in 1912, or the torpedoing of the Cunard liner *Lusitania*, off the coast of Ireland in 1915, the tragedy of the *Princess Sophia* had little staying power outside of residents of Alaska and British Columbia.

In an ironic twist, the Canadian Pacific steamship *Princess Alice* also came alongside Vancouver's Pier D on the jubilant evening of November 11. Buried amid the next day's headlines cheering the end of the war to end all wars was the news that *Princess Alice* — the "Ship of Sorrow" — had brought with her 156 bodies from the *Princess Sophia*, destined for Vancouver, Victoria, and Seattle. It was an enormous amount for a single ship to carry, yet that still represented less than half of the total passengers and crew on board. Owing to the late hour of her arrival, their remains would spend one final evening on the ship before being offloaded at 7:00 a.m. the next day.

For the relatives of the victims, however, closure would be a long and painful road. Relatives had to come from far and wide to identify their loved ones. In some cases identification proved to be a bizarre process. Such was the situation that befell Orton Phillips, a waiter on board the *Princess Sophia*. An American citizen, Phillips had no close relations who could identify his remains, so two Victoria policemen performed the task. Phillips had been arrested in Victoria in August 1918, when he was found to have driven a motor vehicle while under the influence. Unable to pay the fine, he had spent a week in the local jail instead. Three months later the arresting officers had been asked to make the identification. They did, and the story made the next morning's *Victoria Daily Colonist*.

More often than not, however, the stories shared amongst the victims' relatives and friends were the same. Although the names were different, the profound sense of loss experienced by their relatives permeated entire towns and cities, particularly in the rural cities of Alaska and British Columbia. Even larger cities like Vancouver were not immune to the overriding scope of the tragedy. Still reeling from the influenza outbreak that had swept through the Pacific Northwest, gravediggers had difficulty keeping up with the bodies that were being offloaded from the *Princess Alice*.

The sinking of the *Princess Sophia* had devastated entire swaths of the Pacific Northwest, and the region's pain was felt across Canada. In Ottawa Prime Minister Sir Robert Borden wrote that "the shocking completeness of the great tragedy has deeply moved and touched the citizens of the entire Dominion."[9]

In the United States memorial services were held in Seattle and vast swaths of Alaska, though Juneau and Skagway arguably suffered the most. On both sides of the border, the United States and Canada were united in their grief.

If the actual sinking failed to make headlines, the inquiry and subsequent decades of legal wrangling on both sides of the border often did. In Victoria the first days of the Canadian inquiry into the sinking commenced at the start of the New Year, on January 6, 1919. Held before Justice Aulay Morrison and Captain J.D. Macpherson, the inquiry lasted over two months and eventually moved from Victoria to Vancouver to Juneau, Alaska, in order to obtain testimony from every person who had any relevant connection with the ship and its subsequent sinking.

The inquiry was nothing if not thorough, with anyone who bore the slightest connection to the ship being called to testify. Questions ran the gamut from standard ("At what time did you arrive at the wreck?") to absurd. Eager to free Canadian Pacific from any claims of liability that would have cost the company dearly, the company's lawyers went into overdrive. Their efforts were equally matched by lawyers for the victims' families, who took great strides to paint Captain Locke as a drunk, sex-crazed womanizer who frequently invited guests to run wild in his wheelhouse. At various stages he was accused of having been senile, racist, suffering from acute illness, and bouts of rage. The crew of the *Princess Sophia* were painted as young and inexperienced; Canadian Pacific as cheap and unwilling to pay for expensive rescue operations, but more than willing to pony up the cash to recover the gold on board.

These were, of course, gross generalizations, and their only real effect was to drag out an already long and painful legal process. In the end, Justice Morrison's final take on the over seven hundred pages of testimony accumulated during the Canadian inquiry filled just eight pages of text. His conclusion: *Princess Sophia* was lost "through the peril of the sea."[10] With no real evidence as to how or why the ship came to be off course and aground on Vanderbilt Reef, and photographic evidence and eyewitness testimony indicating that rescue was, for the most part, too risky to have been conducted given the weather conditions at the time, Morrison also found that Captain Locke acted prudently in not trying to attempt a more aggressive evacuation of his ship.

Although the inquiry had concluded, by May of 1919 it was becoming apparent that Canadian Pacific's initial efforts to recover bodies that might still be trapped within the wreck were not enough. Diving operations resumed in the spring. A total of eighty-six more victims were found inside the wreck, and their remains were brought to the surface. Their seven-month disappearing act was attributed to strong currents and poor visibility on previous searches.

Around this time the shipping line also decided that the time had come to salvage the wreck of the *Princess Sophia*. Canadian Pacific hired the Deep Sea Salvage Company to raise the wreck, but this, too, brought more unwanted attention. During the winter of 1919 the Deep Sea Salvage Company raised over $40,000 from investors throughout British Columbia and Alaska, dangling the promise of untold rewards that would spill forth from the sunken ship once she was salvaged. This, of course, never came to pass. As the *Whitehorse Weekly Star* alluded several times throughout the winter of 1919–20, the general feeling was that people had been duped. The wreck could not be raised, and most of the items of value (like the Wells-Fargo safe) had already been recovered. By the summer of 1920 the Deep Sea Salvage Company was bankrupt, and with that all talk of salvaging the *Princess Sophia* ceased.

The gold rush never seemed to truly die out in Alaska. Where there was tragedy and despair, profit was not far behind. Public opinion was also largely against Canadian Pacific at the time. To fully appreciate the negative sentiments toward the prosperous rail and shipping line, the modern-day comparison would be legacy airlines like Air Canada or American Airlines. Though nearly a century has passed, our love-hate relationship with the companies that get us where we need to go has changed very little.

In 1921 the American inquiry into the sinking began in earnest. It produced thousands of pages of testimony, many of which contained contradictory testimony and wild, baseless accusations inserted in an attempt to prove the Canadian Pacific Steamship Company's guilt. The sordid tale of the legal wrangling alone was enough to fill a book; proceedings, claims, counter-claims, and petitions of various nature related to the sinking would tie up the process until 1930, when the United States District Court for the Western District of Washington granted Canadian Pacific the limitation of liability the company had requested. In 1932 the United States Circuit Court of Appeals for the Ninth Circuit upheld that decision.

Princess Adelaide sails out of Vancouver through the First Narrows in 1914. She was one of three sister ships to *Princess Sophia*, though parts of her deck layout varied considerably.

Fourteen years after she ran aground on Vanderbilt reef, the legal wrangling surrounding the sinking of the *Princess Sophia* had finally made its long and arduous journey across the finish line. Left in its deadly wake were swaths of anguish, bitter disappointment, and — perhaps most crucially — a deep mistrust of Canadian Pacific.

Even after the dust had settled, some of the most basic questions of the disaster went unanswered. Why had Captain Locke delayed in getting the passengers and crew off in the boats at the first available opportunity? Why had the ship run aground in the first place? Was Captain Locke under pressure from his employers to maintain the ship's published schedule on this crucial final southbound run of the year? Could the rescuers, most of whom anchored or held their ships at an arm's length for days, have done any better? The second guessing of the events that played out between October 23 and October 25, 1918, would be analyzed and scrutinized in the years and decades to come.

Canadian Pacific had expected to make nearly $80,000 in profits from the final run of the *Princess Sophia*; they ended up spending nearly that much paying for the consequences of her sinking. The vast majority went to undertakers; with the line offering to ship victims' remains anywhere in Canada or the United States for free, twenty undertakers from Vancouver to Ottawa and points in between scooped up $54,973.58 of the company's profits. Payment for the ships that had anchored near the stricken *Princess Sophia* and assisted in the rescue tallied $14,892.63. Complimentary tickets for relatives of the bereaved set them back $2,529.78. Flowers alone totalled $130 — nearly $2,000 in modern currency.

In all, not much was left of Canadian Pacific's expected $80,000 profit. The entire disaster set them back $78,074.22. The damage to their reputation, however, was more difficult to pin down. In an effort to wipe the saga from public view, Canadian Pacific destroyed nearly all materials relating to the ship, from brochures to deck plans and publicity photographs. Sadly, this means that some of the only materials available on this beautiful vessel relate directly to the sinking itself. A quick Google search of the term "Princess Sophia" immediately brings up photographs of the ship, stricken in the blinding snow on Vanderbilt Reef. Had more of these early publicity materials survived, perhaps

the story would have ended differently. Should they have been kept, perhaps the ship wouldn't be shrouded in such mystery — and accusations that Canadian Pacific was eager to cover up the whole affair could have been put to rest.

Nearly a century has passed since the tragic events that occurred in Lynn Canal in the dying days of October 1918. Canadian Pacific ships no longer ply the coastal waters of British Columbia and Alaska. The formation of the British Columbia Ferry Corporation in 1960, coupled with the reduction in passenger traffic from Alaska and the introduction of affordable jet airplanes that made flying the faster and more economical choice, sounded the death knell for Canadian Pacific. While newer steamships were built to sail the Pacific Coast, Canadian Pacific seemed to be stuck in its ways, refusing to modernize. Even when Alaska cruising began in earnest out of Vancouver during the 1960s and steadily gained popularity, Canadian Pacific made no real efforts to court the cruising trade. The waters of Alaska became the undisputed stomping grounds of early cruise pioneers in the region like Princess Cruises, which has continually operated in Alaska and British Columbia since their first voyage back in 1969.

Despite the rising increase in cruise passenger traffic, the construction of the new Canada Place cruise terminal in Vancouver and the restoration of Ballantyne Pier farther to the east, Canadian Pacific never made a move to enter the pleasure cruising market in Alaska. Even the company's famous "Multimark" logo, consisting of a red-and-white half moon coupled with a black triangle, was no longer hip or cool. Used from 1968 to 1987, video gamers of the 1980s likened it to the video game character Pac Man, while Carnival Cruise

CANADIAN PACIFIC RAILWAY COMPANY's
STEAMER
PRINCESS SOPHIA

Issued June 3rd, 1912

General arrangement plans for the *Princess Sophia*, as issued to Canadian Pacific agents in 1912.

Present-day Skagway is every bit as busy as the Skagway of days gone by.

Lines famously based their iconic red, blue, and white funnel off that very logo. When Carnival acquired the *Empress of Canada* in 1972, the line simply altered the colours to blue, red, and white, and smoothed out the black triangle. This basic colour arrangement, with its Canadian Pacific heritage, can be seen on every Carnival cruise ship to this day.

Once *Empress of Canada* had been sold to Carnival to become their *Mardi Gras*, it was the end of the line for the steamships division of Canadian Pacific. Coastal service limped along into the 1980s, but soon folded under pressure from BC Ferries, the Washington Marine Group, and the staunch Black Ball Line, which has managed to provide service between Washington State and Victoria using a single ferry — the MV *Coho* — for nearly sixty years.

In 2001 CP Ships, Ltd., was separated from parent company Canadian Pacific, and became its own entity. Four years later, on October 25, 2005 — eighty-seven years to the day of the sinking of the *Princess Sophia* — CP Ships was acquired by TUI AG to be incorporated into their Hapag-Lloyd division for $21.50 USD per share. In 2011 the Canadian Pacific Steamships Limited trade name was officially abandoned. Two years later it popped up in Ontario, Canada, incorporated as the name of an upstart clothing company.

In the end the real tragedy of the *Princess Sophia* may very well be her obscurity. Despite the dozens of cruise ships that sail right past her wreckage as they make their way to and from Skagway, few passengers who visit the region will ever learn of the *Princess Sophia*. Like her wreckage, her memory is kept out of sight and out of view. Books on the ship are few and far between. But inquisitive folks can ask the townspeople in Juneau and Skagway; even if they weren't around when she went down, nearly everyone who has lived there for any length of time has heard of the *Princess Sophia*.

On the corner of Front and Franklin Street in Juneau sits the Triangle Club Bar. It's occupied that site since 1947, and has been quenching the thirst of locals and tourists alike for decades. It's also one of the few places in the Pacific Northwest to actually pay homage to the region's treacherous waters. If you go inside, let your eyes adjust to the darkness, amble up to the bar, order a pint of Alaskan Amber ale, and look over the wall of photos that lines the back left corner of the bar. There, third from the left on the top row — just next to the industrial coffee maker — is a photograph of the *Princess Sophia*, forever perched atop Vanderbilt Reef, waiting for someone to ask who she is. Waiting for someone to tell her story — and the story of the 343 passengers and crew who went down with her on that cold October night.

The final tragedy of the *Princess Sophia* is that her story was allowed to be forgotten.

CHAPTER TWELVE
STAR PRINCESS SAILS ON

He is a professional … he knows where we should be.[1]
— Testimony from officers aboard the *Star Princess* in the NTSB Inquiry

Like the *Princess Sophia* seventy-six years earlier, the grounding of the *Star Princess* quickly evaporated from the headlines — though for very different reasons. In late June 1995 the trial of former footballer and film star O.J. Simpson, for the murder of his ex-wife Nicole Brown Simpson and waiter Ronald Goldman, was still in full swing. By the time *Star Princess* ran aground on Poundstone Rock, Johnnie Cochran was close to belting out his famous "If it doesn't fit, you must acquit"[2] directive to the jury regarding the now-infamous leather glove. The media circus surrounding the event was still catapulting the daily hiccups of the "trial of the century" on to the front page of most North American newspapers.

In July Iraq, under the direction of Saddam Hussein, revealed the full extent of the country's biological warfare capabilities. In August Bill Gates and Microsoft took centre stage with the release of Windows 95. And on the last day of the year, cartoonist Bill Watterson drew the very last strip of *Calvin and Hobbes*. In the age before commercial news networks like CNN careened from one media spectacle to the next, a ship that ran aground in Alaska without causing a single fatality quickly found itself removed from the headlines. After all, stories with a happy ending aren't real news.

Despite the absence of any fatalities, the investigation into the accident would drag on for nearly two years. In March 1997 the National Transportation Safety Board (NTSB) released their full sixty-three-page report into the grounding of the *Star Princess* on Poundstone Rock. A total of $27.1 million dollars' worth of damage had been caused to her hull in the accident, and Princess Cruises was forced to scrub much of her 1995 Alaska season in order to perform necessary repairs.

The NTSB report outlined seventeen factors that contributed to the accident in the early morning hours of June 24, 1995. Summarized, the accident was largely attributed to the fatigued Pilot Nerup, who suffered from sleep apnea leading up to the grounding. The reluctance of the navigational officers and other members of the deck department who were on the bridge that night also played a part in the grounding; by not questioning the actions of the pilot, the officers essentially assumed that as an experienced marine pilot licenced by the state of Alaska, Nerup knew what he was doing and would make any necessary course corrections in due time in order to ensure the safe navigation of the vessel. As one officer put it during his testimony to the NTSB: "he is a professional … he knows where we should be."

In the same way that airline disasters of the time brought increased awareness into the importance of communication between junior and senior crew members — a process known as "crew resource management" — the accident also did much to highlight the ever-changing roles of officers on the bridge of a modern ship. This was particularly true in 1995, when technology straddled an odd combination of analogue and digital devices. *Star Princess*, having been built in 1988 and designed even earlier than that, only exacerbated that gap between proven, existing methods of navigation and the electronic systems that were quickly becoming part of the modern navigator's toolkit. The NTSB concluded that although the watch officers had manually plotted position fixes at 01:14 and again at 01:30, they did not use the data to project the forward path of *Star Princess*. Had they done so they would have seen that in thirty minutes' time their current course would bring them dangerously close to Poundstone Rock. If the officers took the time to fully plot out the track of their vessel they would have undoubtedly notified the pilot, who would have made the appropriate course corrections.

More than anything, the *Star Princess* accident came out of a lack of crew resource management (CRM) procedures on the bridge that night. The idea behind effective CRM came from the aviation industry in the late 1970s, following the crash of United Airlines Flight 173. A scheduled flight from Denver to Portland, Oregon, United 173 had a completely normal flight until the crew lowered the landing gear. When the gear on the Douglas DC-8 came down, it was accompanied by a loud *thump*-ing noise and airframe vibration. The plane experienced abnormal yaw, and the green light indicator that would illuminate when the gear was lowered and locked failed to do so. Unbeknownst to the crew, the gear had fallen and locked into place after the failure of a subsystem, and the additional failure of a secondary system caused the gear lights to not light up in the cockpit. The three crew members on the flight deck that night became so obsessed with solving the landing-gear problem — which, in actuality, had already been solved — that they neglected to monitor their fuel levels, which led to the fuel starvation of the DC-8's four Pratt & Whitney turbofan engines. Ten people died when the plane crashed into a Portland suburb; 179 miraculously survived.[3]

While the aviation industry quickly began adopting the lessons of crew resource management, the marine industry was slower to catch on. Chains of command and the reluctance to question fellow professionals undoubtedly played a role in the grounding of the *Star Princess*. If anything, the *Star Princess* accident was the catalyst for implementing and updating crew resource management procedures across the entire cruise and maritime industry.

In hindsight, it is not difficult to surmise that crew resource management — or the lack thereof — played a substantial role in the grounding of the *Princess Sophia* on Vanderbilt Reef. You have a ship that is short on lookouts sailing through a raging snowstorm in a narrow canal fraught with navigational hazards. An experienced senior captain is in the wheelhouse, in command. The only other officer on the bridge is half his age, commands half his pay, and has half his status. If First Officer Jerry Shaw harboured any doubts about his boss he likely kept them to himself rather than risk a dressing down in front of the ship's quartermaster.

Timing also probably played a role in this willful complacency; turning around and seeking shelter in Haines or even Skagway would have had an enormous knock-on effect to the ship's schedule. The fact that this was *Princess Sophia*'s last journey south for the 1918 season likely had more to do with the decision to press on. Like their passengers, Locke and Shaw were probably more than ready to see the backside of Alaska disappear off their stern. If he had doubts, Captain Locke probably wouldn't have shared them with the younger Jerry Shaw. Shaw, in turn, would be loath to question his commander's skill and leadership. And so both men stood there, peering out into the darkness at the snow that zipped like lightning across the window panes, each hiding their nagging doubts from one another, until shortly after two in the morning of October 23, 1918.

Like a bolt of lightning, clarity came to the men on the bridge of the *Princess Sophia* in the form of a low scraping sound that reverberated through the ship and instantly sealed the fates of those on board.

The only real hope; the one glimmer of light to emanate from those dark days in October nearly a century ago, was that her sinking and the deaths of all those who went down with her serve as a reminder of the power of the sea. Nothing is for naught if it prevents future tragedies.

Today modern navigation systems use computers and global positioning systems to monitor not only the current location of the ship, but also to project its future path. This navigation system displays the number of hours or minutes needed to reach an intended target or waypoint, and can even calculate when approaching vessels — like the *Fair Princess* that threw off Pilot Robert Nerup aboard *Star Princess* that evening — will come abreast of the ship, based on their current speed and heading. Radars mounted in multiple locations on large cruise ships help to "paint" a better picture of obstacles that lie ahead of and around their projected path, even in instances of bad weather and heavy fog. The phrase "crew resource management" has transitioned from myth to standard operating procedure.

Coincidentally, the 1997 release of the NTSB's report coincided with the exit of *Star Princess* from the Princess Cruises fleet. After less than a decade in service, she was transferred to sister company P&O Cruises, where she was based out of Southampton, England, from 1997 until 2003. Known as *Arcadia*, she sported a buff yellow funnel in place of the Princess "sea witch" logo. Change was afoot again in 2003, when the former *Star Princess* became the launch vessel for the short-lived Ocean Village brand. Renamed *Ocean Village* and given a garish new livery of purple and orange cheatlines, Ocean Village was billed as "the cruise for people who don't do cruises." It turned out that most cruisers also didn't do Ocean Village cruises, and by 2010 Ocean Village had become part of P&O Australia. The former *Star Princess* changed names again, this time to *Pacific Pearl*. Repainted with the P&O logo that used to adorn her superstructure, she's since sailed a happy, trouble-free existence year-round in Australia.

In 2002 a new *Star Princess* was completed for Princess Cruises. At 109,000 GRT, she is substantially larger than her predecessor, and is derived from the line's signature *Grand Princess* that first entered service in 1998. Both vessels are still in service today, though the new *Star Princess* experienced her own unfortunate bout of notoriety in 2006, when fire broke out in the early morning hours of March 23 as the ship was sailing off the coast of Montego Bay, Jamaica. An improperly discarded cigarette left smouldering on a balcony sparked a blaze that wiped out nearly one hundred staterooms and led to the death of one passenger from a heart attack. *Star Princess* was sent to Europe for two months of repairs, and re-entered service in May 2006.[4]

Pilot Ronald Joseph Kutz died on July 9, 2002, in Seattle due to severe complications relating to an accident that occurred on June 12 of that year. His notice of death and obituary ran prominently in the *Juneau Empire* on July 16, 2002, and reflected on the many happy years he and his wife, Marilyn, had called Alaska's capital city their home.

For Pilot Robert K. Nerup the aftermath of the *Star Princess* accident was decidedly less kind. Immediately following the grounding, Nerup would testify before the National Transportation Safety Board investigation team that had been sent to Alaska. His attorney, Anchorage-based Bob Richmond, attempted to do damage control to his client's reputation, swiftly refusing the multitude of interview requests coming in from publications in Alaska and afar. His refusal to let Nerup speak only compounded the problems he would face as more details emerged about his past accidents, and his use of the drug Effexor, to treat his depression, at the time of the accident.

In the days that were to follow, Princess Cruises attempted to distance themselves from Nerup, despite the fact that they had apparently expressed no qualms about his performance or capabilities as a marine pilot in the wake of the collision between the *Island Princess* and *Regent Sea* in Skagway harbour in 1991. Princess captains that he had served alongside had come to his defence, testifying to both his exemplary personal and professional attitudes. Nevertheless, Nerup's depression and use of Effexor to manage it were publicly disclosed for the first time, and while the NTSB could find no immediate issues with the Effexor, Nerup's personal problems were dragged to the surface for all to see.

In October 1995 doctors officially diagnosed Nerup with obstructive sleep apnea (OSA). A condition that causes the sufferer to briefly stop breathing for short periods, it is estimated that 1 to 4 percent of the population of the United States suffers from OSA. Research into the condition has shown that men are significantly more likely to develop sleep apnea than women, particularly those men who have crossed over forty years of age. Both male and over forty years of age, Robert Nerup fit the bill. Coupled with the chaotic and changeable watch schedule demanded by his career, his sleep apnea likely left Nerup tired and fatigued — whether the long-time mariner knew it or not. Independent researchers contracted by the NTSB on the subject concluded it was entirely plausible that this sleep apnea played a critical role in Nerup's decision-making abilities on the day of the accident; sleep apnea can often manifest itself with symptoms that include morning headaches, excessive daytime sleepiness, depression, intellectual impairment, and memory deficit. Whether he knew it or not, Robert Nerup's sleep apnea, depression, and treatment for it likely affected his decision-making processes on the night of the accident.

Not that Nerup is entirely to blame. For the first time ever in a marine accident, transcripts from the ship's voyage data recorder (VDR) were used in an NTSB investigation. Much like the "black box" in an airplane, the VDR records the parameters of all relevant technical systems on board a ship, including speed, heading, current location transmitted by global positioning satellites (GPS), and even data collected from the four radars installed aboard *Star Princess*. Following the accident they were sent to London, England, where they were played back for NTSB investigators in December 1995. From those playbacks, investigators were able to reconstruct the actual track of the *Star Princess* from the radar, gyro, and GPS coordinates contained within.

Crucially, the VDR also contains an audio track recorded from a handful of live microphones located throughout the navigation bridge. When the NTSB reviewed the tracks, the audio quality was poor. Princess Cruises, to their credit, promptly furnished the NTSB with transcripts of all conversations that took place on the navigation bridge

between 01:02 and 01:59 on the morning of June 23, 1995. The discussion on the bridge between the officers on duty and the pilot in the run up to the collision revolved mainly around their family relationships and issues, and personal grooming habits. In their report, the NTSB investigators noted that "the matters discussed by the watch officers and pilot were not of a navigational nature and were not related to shipboard duties."[5] Not a single officer on the bridge of the *Star Princess* questioned Nerup's decision-making process. They were talking about how they like their hair cut, and where their wives and kids were.

The stigma of the *Star Princess* proved to be impossible for Robert Nerup to shake. On April 2, 1996, he surrendered his Alaska marine pilot's licence following a decision and settlement by the State of Alaska. Bearing the identification number eighty-three, it was issued on December 9, 1980, and expired on the last day of 1996. His file was permanently marked with a clause, issued in all capitals:

LICENSE SURRENDERED — WILL NEVER AGAIN APPLY FOR MARINE PILOT LICENSE OF ANY SORT ISSUED BY THE STATE OF ALASKA.[6]

He never went back to sea.

Cruise ships have increased rapidly in size since 1995. Vessels that were once considered large — like the former *Star Princess* — now barely qualify as midsize. Capacities are on the rise, too, with the largest ships currently sailing in Alaska capable of carrying nearly four thousand passengers. They are, first and foremost, a safe, reliable, enjoyable way to see Alaska. In many ways, they tend to mimic their aviation counterparts in terms of safety, but also in scope and scale when something goes awry. In recent years, events like the sinking of the *Costa Concordia* and the loss of power aboard the *Carnival Triumph* have illustrated that modern cruise ships, like any technology, are far from infallible. But to sail through Lynn Canal today on one of these floating technological marvels can be as deceiving as it was on that blustery night in October 1918 when *Princess Sophia* steamed toward her inevitable fate. In their final report into the grounding of the *Star Princess*, the NTSB noted that the greatest danger in Alaska may very well be the one thing that is entirely out of human control: mother nature.

Considering the unforgiving nature of the Alaskan marine environment, with its deep, cold waters and rocky shores, and the remoteness of the areas of operation, an accident caused by the poor performance of a pilot cannot be tolerated. Too many lives are at risk.[7]

NOTES

INTRODUCTION

1. *Official Inquiry into the Loss of the* Princess Sophia, *1919*, Library and Archives Canada, lac_mikan_165657; R.G. 42, Volume 355, 8.
2. "Sport Fish Report For the Week of July 28," *Juneau Empire*, http://juneauempire.com/outdoors/2014-08-01/sport-fish-report-week-july-28, accessed November 23, 2014.

CHAPTER 1: THE RUSH TO SKAGWAY

1. Jason Moore, "Cruise Companies Fret New Water Standards," CLIA Alaska, www.cliaalaska.org/2008/04/cruise-companies-fret-new-water-standards, accessed March 12, 2013.
2. Pierre Berton, *The Wild Frontier: More Tales from the Remarkable Past* (Toronto: Doubleday Canada, 2012).
3. *The Chicago Record 1897*, 97.
4. "2007 Hassler Expedition — Last Days," National Oceanic & Atmospheric Administration, http://sanctuaries.noaa.gov/maritime/expeditions/hassler/last_days.html, accessed February 28, 2015.
5. Berton, *The Wild Frontier*.
6. J. Bernard Moore, *Skagway in Days Primeval* (Skagway, AK: Lynn Canal Publishing, 1963, 1997), 186.
7. Ibid., 184.
8. Pierre Berton, *Klondike: The Last Great Gold Rush 1896–1899* (Toronto: Anchor Canada, 2001), 238–39.
9. Ross Anderson, "The Dawson City Gold Rush Had its Own Bill Gates," *Seattle Times*, July 16, 1997.
10. "Klondike Gold Rush," National Park Service, www.nps.gov/klgo/historyculture/dyea.htm, accessed September 10, 2014.
11. "2007 Hassler Expedition — Last Days," National Oceanic & Atmospheric Administration, http://sanctuaries.noaa.gov/maritime/expeditions/hassler/last_days.html, accessed February 28, 2015.

CHAPTER 2: "A SLOW TRIP THROUGH ALASKA"

1. Betty O'Keefe and Ian MacDonald, *The Final Voyage of the* Princess Sophia (Victoria: Heritage House Publishing, 1998), 46.

2. Ibid., 62.

3. Ken Coates and Bill Morrison, *The Sinking of the* Princess Sophia (Fairbanks, AK: University of Alaska Press, 1991), 12.

4. "The Princess Sophia Is the Largest-Engined Vessel That Ever Was Built on the Cart," *Paisley Gazette*, February 1912.

5. "1005 Cook St," Victoria Heritage Foundation, www.victoriaheritagefoundation.ca/HReg/Fairfield/Cook1005.html, accessed October 17, 2014.

6. "William Gardner Gabie," Skagway Stories, www.skagwaystories.org/2011/01/page/3, accessed September 13, 2014.

7. "The White Pass Hospital & Dr. Dahl," *Skagway News*, www.skagwaynews.com/alaskan2013.html, accessed September 13, 2014.

8. United States Court of Appeals Case #6390, I.M. BRACE vs. CANADIAN PACIFIC, 433–38.

9. Ibid., 83.

10. "Inventory and Survey of Historic Shipwreck Sites," City of Juneau, September 1992, 29–36.

11. Dermot Cole, *Historic Fairbanks: An Illustrated History* (Fairbanks, AK: Fairbanks Chamber of Commerce, 2002), 115.

12. "Wells Fargo: Here For Alaskans, Now and In the Future," The Alliance, http://alaskaalliance.com/wells-fargo-here-for-alaskans-now-and-in-the-future, accessed October 18, 2014.

13. Currency & Inflation Converter, Dollar Times, www.dollartimes.com/inflation/inflation.php?amount=35&year=1918, accessed February 2, 2014.

CHAPTER 3: THE *STAR PRINCESS* SETS SAIL

1. "Obituary: Ronald J. Kutz," *Juneau Empire*, July 16, 2002, http://juneauempire.com/stories/071602/obi_kutz.html, accessed January 7, 2015.

2. "Marine Pilot for Cruise Ship Had Previous Accident in SE," *Daily Sitka Sentinel*, June 29, 1995, www.newspapers.com/newspage/24540624, accessed January 7, 2015.

3. "Two Cruise Ships Collide in Skagway, Only Minor Injuries Are Reported," *The Argus Press*, May 28, 1991, http://news.google.com/newspapers?nid=1988&dat=19910528&id=lkEiAAAAIBAJ&sjid=Ta0FAAAAIBAJ&pg=2238,2171695, accessed January 8, 2015.

4. "Ships Due Here for Collision Repairs," *Seattle Times*, May 29, 1991, http://community.seattletimes.nwsource.com/archive/?date=19910529&slug=1286062, accessed January 8, 2015.

5. "Accident Won't Affect Schedule," JOC, June 5, 1991, www.joc.com/maritime-news/maritime-briefs_19910605.html, accessed January 8, 2015.

CHAPTER 4: THE STORM

1. *Victoria Daily Colonist*, April 5, 6, 7, 1918.

2. Coates and Morrison, *The Sinking of the* Princess Sophia, 53.

3. *Official Inquiry into the Loss of the* Princess Sophia, 454.

4. Ibid., 456.

5. Moore, *Skagway in Days Primeval*, 92–95.

6. "Reports of Captain L.A. Beardslee, U.S. Navy, Relative to Affairs in Alaska, and the Operations of the U.S.S. Jamestown, Under His Command, While In the Waters of that Territory" (1882), U.S. Library of Congress, https://ia601501.us.archive.org/15/items/reportsofcaptain00unit/reportsofcaptain00unit.pdf, accessed October 20, 2014.

7. "The Grounding of the *Princess May*," *Silodrome Gasoline Culture*, http://silodrome.com/grounding-princess-may, accessed February 2, 2014.

8. *Official Inquiry into the Loss of the* Princess Sophia.

CHAPTER 5: THE TURN

1. National Transportation Safety Board Report, "Grounding of the Liberian Passenger Ship *Star Princess* on Poundstone Rock, Lynn Canal, Alaska, June 23, 1995," 1997, 55.

CHAPTER 6: THE ACCIDENT

1. *United States Court of Appeals Case #6390, I.M. BRACE vs. CANADIAN PACIFIC*, "Brief of Appellees," 1919, 15.

2. Ibid., 16.

3. Ibid., 16.

4. Coates and Morrison, *The Sinking of the* Princess Sophia, 173.

5. *Official Inquiry into the Loss of the* Princess Sophia, 457.

6. Ibid., 89.

7. Coates and Morrison, *The Sinking of the* Princess Sophia, 172.

8. Ibid., 171.

9. *Official Inquiry into the Loss of the* Princess Sophia, 102.

10. Ibid., 106.

11. Ibid., 466.

12. Ibid., 39.

13. Ibid., 42.

14. Ibid., 467.

15. Coates and Morrison, *The Sinking of the* Princess Sophia, 172–73.

16. *Official Inquiry into the Loss of the* Princess Sophia, 106.

17. Ibid., 106.

18. Ibid., 109.

19. Ibid., 55.

20. Log, Diary of Governor of Alaska Thomas Riggs, Jr., July 8, 1918–December 25, 1919, 37–52, http://library.alaska.gov/hist/hist_docs/docs/asl_ms273_1_1918-1919_transcript.pdf, accessed October 25, 2014.

21. Ibid.

22. "Cannery Tender," Lake Union Virtual Museum, www.lakeunionhistory.org/Cannery_Tender.html, accessed October 25, 2014.

CHAPTER 7: THE TURN

1. National Transportation Safety Board Report, "Grounding of the Liberian Passenger Ship *Star Princess…*," 7.

2. Ibid., 7.

CHAPTER 8: STRANDED ON THE ROCKS

1. *Official Inquiry into the Loss of the* Princess Sophia, 184

2. Ibid.

3. Ibid., 5.

4. Ibid., 25.

5. Coates and Morrison, *The Sinking of the* Princess Sophia, 172.

6. Ibid.

7. Ibid., 173.

8. Ibid.

9. *United States Court of Appeals Case #6390, I.M. BRACE vs. CANADIAN PACIFIC*, 24.

10. *Official Inquiry into the Loss of the* Princess Sophia, 64.

11. Ibid., 67.

12. Ibid., 460.

13. Coates and Morrison, *The Sinking of the* Princess Sophia, 173.

14. Ibid.

15. *Official Inquiry into the Loss of the* Princess Sophia, 62.

16. *United States Court of Appeals Case #6390, I.M. BRACE vs. CANADIAN PACIFIC*, 25.

17. *Official Inquiry into the Loss of the* Princess Sophia, 43–44.

18. Ibid., 149–50.

19. *United States Court of Appeals Case #6390, I.M. BRACE vs. CANADIAN PACIFIC*, 27.

20. *Official Inquiry into the Loss of the* Princess Sophia, 65.

21. Ibid.

22. Ibid., 66.

23. United States Court of Appeals Case #6390, I.M BRACE vs. CANADIAN PACIFIC, 27.

24. *Official Inquiry into the Loss of the* Princess Sophia, 151.

25. Ibid.

CHAPTER 9: BEACHING THE *STAR PRINCESS*

1. National Transportation Safety Board Report, "Grounding of the Liberian Passenger Ship *Star Princess*…," 11–12.

2. Ibid.

3. Ibid., 12.

CHAPTER 10: THOSE LAST MINUTES

1. *United States Court of Appeals Case #6390, I.M. BRACE vs. CANADIAN PACIFIC*, 27.

2. *Official Inquiry into the Loss of the* Princess Sophia, 67–68.

3. Ibid., 68.

4. Ibid., 69.

CHAPTER 11: AFTERMATH

1. *United States Court of Appeals Case #6390, I.M. BRACE vs. CANADIAN PACIFIC*, 28.

2. Log, Diary of Governor of Alaska Thomas Riggs, Jr.

3. *Official Inquiry into the Loss of the* Princess Sophia, 476.

4. Ibid., 477.

5. Ibid., 84.

6. Ibid., 82.

7. Ibid., 83.

8. Ibid., 88.

9. Coates and Morrison, *The Sinking of the* Princess Sophia, 127.

10. Ibid., 145.

CHAPTER 12: *STAR PRINCESS* SAILS ON

1. National Transportation Safety Board Report, "Grounding of the Liberian Passenger Ship *Star Princess*…," 7.

2. "If It Doesn't Fit, You Must Acquit," CNN, September 28, 1995, www.cnn.com/US/OJ/daily/9-27/8pm, accessed March 4, 2015.

3. National Transportation Safety Board, "Aircraft Accident Report NTSB AAR-79-7 UNITED AIRLINES INC., McDonnel-Douglas DC-8-61, N8082U, Portland, Oregon, December 28, 1978," 1–10.

4. Marine Accident Investigation Branch, "Report on the Investigation of the Fire On Board STAR PRINCESS off Jamaica; 23 March 2006," 17.

5. National Transportation Safety Board Report, "Grounding of the Liberian Passenger Ship *Star Princess*…," 24.

6. "Professional License Details — Robert K. Nerup," State of Alaska/Commerce, www.commerce.state.ak.us/occ/OccSearch/Detail.cfm?board=MAR&LicType=M&LicNum=83, accessed January 7, 2015.

7. National Transportation Safety Board Report, "Grounding of the Liberian Passenger Ship *Star Princess*…," 37.

NOTES ON SOURCES

Considering how little about the *Princess Sophia* is in the public consciousness, a surprising amount of information relating to the shipwreck exists to this day. The primary sources of information I relied upon were the Canadian and American inquiries into the sinking. The *Official Inquiry into the Loss of the* Princess Sophia, *1919*, is now conveniently available online, and contains hundreds of pages of first-hand accounts. Another, even more extensive, resource is the American inquiry, *United States Court of Appeals Case #6390, I.M. BRACE vs. CANADIAN PACIFIC*. Much of it repeats the information present in the Canadian inquiry, but American investigators pressed witnesses repeatedly and with a kind of force not generally present in the Canadian inquiry.

I also drew upon two other contemporary sources, namely Bill Morrison and Ken Coates' excellent *Sinking of the* Princess Sophia, and Betty O'Keefe and Ian MacDonald's *The Final Voyage of the* Princess Sophia. For a portrait of Skagway and Alaska during the beginning of the gold rush, J. Bernard Moore's *Skagway in Days Primeval* was absolutely invaluable. It turns out some things in Skagway never change: the mosquitoes were just as bad in 1887 as they are today. You can visit Moore's homestead in Skagway, and see the desk where he penned his memoirs. He seems like a neat guy who, regrettably, suffered through a difficult marriage and lost most of his money in the years after he left Skagway.

Another invaluable source of information came from Lea Edgar, librarian and archivist at the Vancouver Maritime Museum, who furnished me with entire file folders filled with old newspaper cuttings, letters, archival photographs, and other materials that have been slowly but steadily collected and rounded up by people across the country over the years. It is from these archives that a faded, unclear photocopy of *Princess Sophia*'s general arrangement plans were found, along with numerous press clippings relating to her launch in Scotland and subsequent entry into service on the west coast.

With my hands strapped into latex gloves that seemed to be two sizes too small, I slowly worked my way through the vast mountain of information until I arrived at a letter penned by Captain Locke on January 2, 1918, and mailed that afternoon. Written on Canadian Pacific stationery, it told me quite a bit about Leonard Locke the man: his handwriting was impeccable. Flawless, even. This was the work of a cautious, measured man. Ten months later, those very qualities would work against the experienced mariner in ways he could have never anticipated.

Of course, except for the testimony of the would-be rescuers and the various wireless messages that were passed among the ships, we really don't know exactly what happened aboard the *Princess Sophia* in those last hours on Vanderbilt Reef. I made a conscious choice to attempt to portray what was happening on the ship; who was doing what, where people were. Based on what is known about the folks on board the ship from the friends, colleagues, and loved ones they left behind, and the testimony of people like Selmer Jacobson, who actually dove down to the wreck in the weeks following the sinking, I felt I could draw some reasonable (and careful) conclusions about where people were, and what they were doing, by connecting the dots between these known facts. It's not difficult to imagine, for example, that Walter Barnes would have remained in or near the cargo holds for most of the ordeal, given how attached he was to his beloved horse, Old Billy.

I also made a conscious choice to avoid the trial and to "time jump" as little as possible. The trial was so extensive and filled with information that an entire book could be written just on those proceedings alone. Those hours up on the reef were what fascinated me most. Therefore, I've focused more on the facts surrounding *Princess Sophia*'s journey from Skagway, and the plight of her would-be rescuers.

There is also no substitute for actually travelling to Alaska. Over the course of writing this book I made four trips north, travelling to Skagway and Juneau multiple times on numerous ships in my attempts to sail the waters of Lynn Canal as much as possible. It's a curious stretch of water, and the more I sailed it the more it unsettled me. The winds that whip down that canal, from the ghost town of Dyea, can catch you off guard even in the middle of July.

For those who are travelling to southeast Alaska, there are some fabulous bookstores that still dedicate themselves to providing interesting publications on the unique history of Alaska. They are:

- Hearthside Books: 254 Front Street, Juneau, Alaska
- Old Harbor Books: 201 Lincoln Street, Sitka, Alaska
- Parnassus Books: 105 Stedman Street, Ketchikan, Alaska.
- Skaguay News Depot & Books: 264 Broadway Street, Skagway, Alaska

Finally, I'd be remiss if I didn't thank those who gave their encouragement, lent a hand, or just humoured me as I stayed up until all hours sifting through articles and redrawing deck plans. Special thanks for their kind support and assistance during the production of this book — which is a bit like giving birth to a child — go to: Brad Ball, Margaret Bryant, Camille Drevillon, Carrie Gleason, Cheryl Hawley, Peter Knego, Aileen Laurel, Karen McMullin, Kimberly Plumridge, Adrian Raeside, Cheyenne Sanchez, Maureen and Peter Saunders, Alicia Saunders, and Caitlyn Stewart.

INDEX